HIGH COUNTRY BREEZE

BY
ED ROBINSON

Copyright 2018 by Ed Robinson

All rights reserved. No part of this work shall be reproduced in any manner without the written permission of the publisher.

Published by Leap of Faith Publications

This is a work of fiction. Any actual person or place mentioned is used fictitiously. Though some of my work is based on my real life experiences, most of it is a product of my imagination.

This is dedicated to the hardy souls of the High Country. Anyone can appreciate the beauty of the area, but it takes a special breed to live here.

The High Country

The term refers to the higher elevations in Northern North Carolina's Blue Ridge Mountains. It is best known as a winter sports haven, but towns like Boone and Blowing Rock delight in every season.

The town of Banner Elk sits at the base of several mountains. Sugar and Beech Mountains each have world-class ski resorts. Grandfather Mountain is kept natural and hosts visitors from all over the region.

After skiing, hiking is the premier pastime of locals and tourists alike. Stunning scenery can be found on hundreds of trails and climbs throughout the area. Other popular attractions are Linville Falls and Linville Caverns, just off the Blue Ridge Parkway.

Winters can be severe, with the highest peaks seeing over one-hundred inches of snowfall each year. Mountain roads that seem fun during nice weather become treacherous when covered with snow and ice.

Waterfalls are abundant, and hiking to view them is the most popular fair weather activity of all.

One

They found his body at the bottom of the old mill pond's spillway. The fall had only been twenty feet, but his body lay mangled in the rocks of the Elk River. The area was heavily trafficked, so he was found the first thing the next morning. Billy Buck likely suffered for hours before his death.

It was quickly labeled a suicide. Billy was a geeky kid prone to depression and dark thoughts. He'd been ostracized as a student at Lees-McRae College in Banner Elk. He didn't fit in with the cool kids or the jocks. He'd been teased relentlessly until he killed himself at the age of eighteen.

The story briefly caused a stir in the High Country but was soon forgotten. I never gave it a second thought until Brody got a call from the boy's parents. We'd recently formed a legal partnership and opened our own agency, Creekside Investigations. With that decision came the purchase of shiny new smartphones, something I'd resisted for many years.

The salesman at the AT&T store in Boone had set us up with a business account so that our names weren't attached. That's what convinced me to finally give in. No one that might want to find me could know that Creekside Investigations was actually Brody and me. We could remain anonymous in the digital world, as long as we were careful.

Darla and Frank Buck didn't believe that their son had killed himself. They readily admitted to his quirks but were convinced that suicide was impossible. They'd made their pitch to campus security and the Banner Elk Police Department, but the case had officially been closed. We were the only private investigators in town, so they turned to us for help. We met them at the Banner Elk Café for coffee and conversation.

"I'm sure most parents think the same as we do," Darla said. "But we can't let this go without trying. Billy had his dark moments, but there is no way in hell that he'd quit on life like that."

"He would have called us or come home," Frank said. "We were still a close family. He always came to us with his troubles."

"I'd like to help," I said. "But I know none of the details of what happened. Getting information out of college kids might be a tough gig for me."

"Please," Darla said. "You've got to see if you can find out what really happened. We don't care how long it takes."

Brody had been listening and observing without speaking. She had a talent for sizing people up. She apparently decided that Billy's parents were sincere in their belief.

"The campus is small," she said. "Kids will talk. I think we can get to the bottom of this."

"God bless you," said Darla, getting up to hug Brody.

"About our fee," I said to Frank. "If the investigation drags on it could get expensive."

"We don't have a lot of money," Frank said. "But we will do whatever it takes. We'll take out a second mortgage if we have to."

Brody shot me a look. This would be our first official job, and we weren't hurting for money.

"We'll work it out," I said. "Maybe design a payment plan."

"That's very kind of you," Frank said. "Much appreciated."

"We'll need much more information about Billy," I said. "But I don't want to talk here. Can we come to your place? Maybe tomorrow?"

"Sure thing," Frank said. "You know Old Shelby Road off Henry Fork?"

"Can't say that I do," I said. "But we can find it with a house number."

"It's the only farmhouse between Heartwood and the river," he said. "You can't miss it."

Brody was thumbing her phone, looking at a map. She'd quickly made good use of our new technology.

"Got it," she said. "One o'clock okay?"

"Make it noon, and I'll fix lunch," Darla said.
"Great, thanks," I said. "We'll see you then."

That night we tried to come up with a game plan. I had no idea what type of strategy we could use.

"I'm way out of my comfort zone with this," I told Brody. "I don't even know where to begin."

"I could sense that back at the café," she said. "But I didn't have the heart to tell them no."

"Then you can figure out how to proceed," I said. "You have the lead on our first semi-paying job. Let me know when Red and I can help."

"We start hanging out where the college kids go," she said. "Every employee in that café looks like a college kid, for starters. We'll figure out where else they frequent, ask around. See where it leads us."

"A fifty-six-year-old man is a fish out of water on a college campus," I said. "Those girls all look twelve-years-old to me."

"I thought you'd jump at the chance to be around cute young coeds," she said.

"I try hard not to be a dirty old man," I told her. "My days with cute co-eds are long over. Besides, I haven't seen one girl down there as pretty as you."

"Flattery will get you everywhere," she said. "But let's see what else Frank and Darla have to say before we go off half-cocked."

"There must be more than a feeling that the kid wouldn't kill himself," I suggested. "They wouldn't seek outside help otherwise, especially since they don't appear to have much money."

"We'll find out tomorrow," she said. "They'll be more comfortable at home than they were today. We'll eat Darla's sandwiches and let them talk."

"I'll concentrate on Frank," I said. "You ladies chat away."

Brody spent the rest of the night researching Lees-McRae College. Before she logged off, I asked her to check into suicide rates among college students. We soon learned that the number of suicides among that age group had dramatically increased in recent years. Females attempted the act more frequently than males, but males were much more successful. It had become the second leading cause of death for college students, behind traffic accidents.

I found the statistic surprising, but I had little comprehension of what drove people to kill themselves. I'd not flirted with the idea once, even during the worst of times. Various articles that we read discussed kids being away from home and their support system while dealing with all the stresses of a new life, workload, lack of sleep and exposure to drugs and alcohol. For some, moving away to attend college was more than they could handle, both psychologically and emotionally.

Billy Buck was only an hour from home, and allegedly still close to his parents. If he didn't fit in at college, he probably hadn't fit in at high school either. If he were too weak to deal with it, he wouldn't have chosen to go to college in the first place. Why subject yourself to four more years of ridicule? I was developing questions in my mind to ask his parents the next day. What was his course of study? What were his interests? Did he have girlfriends, or any friends at all? Why Lees-McRae?

I got tired of our internet searches, so I left Brody to continue while I took Red outside for a while. We played fetch for thirty minutes. He would have played all night if I let him. He loved being outside and running around. Inside the cabin, he mostly laid around. He needed some outside time now and then.

Brody had gathered some background on Lees-McCrae while I was playing with the dog. It held the distinction of having the highest elevation of any college east of the Mississippi. It was a private school affiliated with the Presbyterian Church. It was founded as an all-female high school in 1899 by Reverend Edgar Tufts. An all-male branch was founded in 1907 in nearby Plumtree, North Carolina. The Plumtree facility was destroyed by fire in 1927, leading the two schools to merge. After the merge, the high school program was phased out, and the institute was renamed the Lees-McRae College, an accredited, coed, junior college.

It was granted four-year status in 1990. The school participates in most major sports programs on the Division II level and boasts one of the best soccer programs in the country. Alumni include several professional football players, MLS Soccer players, a PGA Tour golfer, professional cyclists, and a bombardier on the *Enola Gay*. The four-hundred-acre campus was the mainstay of downtown Banner Elk.

Frank and Darla Buck were good Christian farmers who entrusted their child to a Presbyterian school close to home. Somehow, he ended up dead before the end of his freshman year. Everyone in authority was convinced that it was suicide. We'd been hired to find out if that was true. I almost hoped that it was, because if it wasn't, then someone had killed him. Our little inquiry would become another murder case. I wasn't sure I was ready for that, but I couldn't turn back. Brody and I both had empathy for the Bucks. Their hearts were broken. We were all they had.

The next morning we drove to Boone and took 321 through Blowing Rock and Lenoir. Near Hickory, we turned west on 40 until we came to Old Shelby Road. Brody directed me using her phone until we came to the old farmhouse. The driveway was dirt, and the side yards were a collection of rusted farm equipment and dead vehicles. Though cluttered, it was clean. There was no garbage or junk, just tools of the trade in various states of repair. The drive took us to the back of the house, where we saw cows and horses in a pasture. The main barn was devoid of paint but still looked structurally sound. The house paint was badly faded and peeling in spots. It was hard to see how this family could afford to send their son to college.

Darla was on the back porch before we got out of the car. She rang a bell hanging from the eaves, just like Little House on the Prairie. Frank emerged from the barn, ready for lunch. We were seated in the kitchen and plates were placed in front of us. BLT sandwiches were on the menu, along with potato salad. Brody and I had skipped breakfast to make sure we'd be hungry. It was a good plan because the food was excellent. I suspected that most of the ingredients came right off their farm.

We carried on a pleasant conversation until I felt the time was right to push the subject.

"Can you be more specific about your certainty?" I asked. "I mean that Billy wouldn't consider suicide?"

"He was happy," Darla said. "He was seeing a girl."

"He had a girlfriend?" I asked. "That's important. Who was she?"

"Her name is Kate," Frank said. "Billy described her as out of his league."

"In what way?" I asked.

"He said she was gorgeous and popular," Frank responded. "He didn't know why she'd go out with him, but they'd been on two dates. We never got to meet her."

"Did Billy have girlfriends in high school?" Brody asked.

"Not a one," Darla said. "He was awkward around girls."

"Listen," Frank said. "Let's face it. The boy wasn't attractive or athletic. He was a dork for the most part. He liked to read all the time. If he ever had the slightest interest in girls, I didn't know about it."

"You still spoke with him often?" Brody asked.

"He talked to me more than Frank," Darla said. "Bit of a momma's boy I suppose."

"I've got work to do around here," Frank said. "The boy wasn't much help, but I didn't push him about it. He was more into his studies and his books than this farm."

"That's why we scrimped and saved to send him to college," Darla said. "We thought he might find a purpose there."

"What did he want to be?" Brody asked. "Did he have a major?"

"He hadn't declared yet," Darla said. "He was taking English Literature and Journalism. I think he wanted to be a writer someday."

"That would have suited him," Frank said. "Always had his nose in a book. Didn't care about sports or much of anything else."

"Lees-McRae is a liberal arts school with a Christian background," Darla said. "We never dreamed something like this would happen."

"We thought it was his best shot to make something of himself," Frank said. "He'd never amount to anything if he stayed around here."

"We're both terribly sorry for what happened," Brody said. "I can't imagine losing a child."

"We're managing the best we know how," Darla said. "We'll be okay, eventually. It would sure help if you could prove he didn't kill himself. Suicide is a cardinal sin."

"Did Billy ever listen to music that you didn't approve of?" I asked. "Did you ever suspect drug use? Violent video games?"

"The only thing he ever had on the radio was talk shows," Darla said. "We wouldn't allow video games, and we never thought he was smoking dope or doing any drugs. He was an introvert, content to stay home and read his books."

"What kind of stuff did he read?" I asked.

"Anything he could get his hands on," she said. "I'd take him down to the Salvation Army and Goodwill so he could sift through the cheap paperbacks. He liked old science fiction mostly, but also political stuff, from either side of the aisle."

"He'd read anything that a public figure wrote," Frank said. "He admired thinkers. Fancied himself one."

"No bias right or left?" I asked.

"He wanted to know what both sides were thinking," he said. "Didn't comment much to me about it, but we don't talk politics in this house."

"Do you listen to music?" I asked.

"Old country on the tractor or out in the barn," he said. "TV is usually on in here. I like to see the local news. We don't have cable."

"What's this got to do with anything?" Darla asked.

"I'm trying to get a feel for who Billy was," I said. "The pretty girl is an anomaly."

"We saw it as an important breakthrough," Darla said. "Thought it might bring him out of his shell."

"Maybe she told him she didn't want to see him anymore," I said.

"Our boy didn't kill himself, Mr. Breeze," she said. "That's why we came to you."

"I understand," I said. "Sorry."

"The girl shouldn't be hard to find," Brody said. "Kate, right?"

"That's what he told us," Frank said. "Like I told you, we never met her."

"It's a place to start," Brody said. "Thank you for lunch."

"Great potato salad," I said. "Can't recall having better."

"You're too kind," Darla said.

"We'll be in touch soon," Brody told her. "We may have more questions, but we'll get right to work on this."

"Thank you both," Frank said.

"One more thing," I said. "Did he say where they went on their dates?"

"Got pizza someplace within walking distance," Frank said. "We're not familiar with the town."

"It's something," I said. "We'll figure it out."

We drove back home and kicked around a few ideas. The Banner Elk Café served pretty good pizza, and it was just blocks from campus. It seemed like a college kid hangout to us. There was a diner even closer, but I didn't think they served pizza. Neither of us had a clue what establishments were within the campus itself. We'd have to walk around and scope it out.

Instead of going straight home, I drove us into Banner Elk. We parked by the millpond and walked to the spillway. There was a wooden bridge over the Elk River that led to a trail. We took that trail, which led to student housing on the backside of the Lees-McRae campus. We'd failed to ask where Billy lived. We knew where he had died.

We stopped into the Banner Elk Café on the way home and ordered a pizza. We asked our waitress if she had known Billy Buck. She said she had not, but that his death was a terrible thing. She was in a hurry, and we didn't get a chance to ask her any more questions. We heard no talk of the incident among the random conversations in the café. It was like it never happened.

We spent half an hour walking the outskirts of the campus proper. We noticed an on-campus bar called Wily's that served beer and wine along with Starbucks coffee. We didn't go in. Brody thought we'd need a good reason and may be asked for student ID to enter. That made sense to me, so I deferred to her judgment. She vowed to check into it later.

The investigation was young, but we felt that we'd taken a few steps in the right direction. We'd put in the footwork and hours, and eventually, we'd find the girl and some other kids who knew Billy. If there was foul play involved, maybe we could get someone to talk. We remained open to the possibility that the police had it right, but our job was to make certain of that, or disprove it if we could.

Two

Brody was right about Wily's. We needed to be students or faculty to enter. She made a few calls until she got a meeting with the head of campus security. She explained that we were licensed private investigators acting on behalf of Billy Buck's parents. We just wanted to ask a few questions to random students to satisfy our obligation. She got us a meeting with him the next day.

Hank Carter was an older gentleman but still in good shape. He was an ex-cop whose retirement wasn't quite enough to cover his expenses. He'd worked as a security guard at Lees-McRae long enough to earn the top spot. He wasn't happy about our investigation.

"I may not be a real cop anymore," he said. "But I have an obligation to the college. What is it that you're trying to accomplish here?"

"The boy's parents begged us to look into his death further," Brody said. "They aren't convinced it was a suicide."

"That call was made by the Banner Elk PD," he said. "I was on the scene before them, but they examined the body and questioned people close to the boy."

"It's not our intention to undermine their authority," she said. "We have clients that we need to satisfy. We just want to ask around, talk to some of those students, and write up our report."

"So you can get paid," he said. "I'm inclined to allow it if you promise not to rock the boat around here."

"We don't anticipate that," Brody said. "But we won't know until we complete our inquiries."

"Would it be possible to get a list of names of those interviewed by the police?" I asked.

"I didn't say I would help you," he said. "Just let you ask around."

"That's fine," said Brody. "We won't tax your loyalties."

"Everybody's got a job to do," he said. "I answer to the folks who sign my paycheck, same as you."

"Do we need some sort of paperwork to get on campus?" I asked. "Especially into Wily's."

"I've got visitor tags for you," he said. "Don't get them wet and they should last for a week or two."

"When the tags melt we're done?" I asked.

"Something like that," he said. "I can't give you an unlimited timeframe, or access. Do what you can and move onto something else."

"Understood," I said. "Is two weeks enough, Brody?"

"If it doesn't rain," she said. "I'd like to reserve the right to ask for more time if the situation calls for it."

"Can't stop you from asking," Hank said.

Our visitor passes were cardboard tags hanging from a lanyard — the green and gold school colors made for a gaudy necklace. There was the image of a bobcat in the lower right corner. We now had begrudging permission to roam the campus, at least until the passes disintegrated. We went to the campus bar first and wasted our money on Starbucks coffee. We sat and observed the students interact. I didn't see one girl that I'd describe as gorgeous, but Billy's taste may have been different from mine. We didn't hear the name Kate mentioned.

After a while, it became evident that the kids weren't speaking freely near us. We didn't belong there. Getting them to talk to us seemed impossible.

"Let's go," Brody said. "We need to rethink our approach."

"Clearly," I said. "Where to?"

"Someplace to laminate these ridiculous visitor badges," she said.

Brody used her new phone to look up what we needed. There was only one place in Banner Elk that could help us. It was a shipping depot called Wraps on Tynecastle Highway. The grumpy clerk wasn't thrilled with our request, but he took our money and encased our passes in plastic.

"That should buy us some time," Brody said.

"Or piss off old Hank," I said.

"Maybe I should go back by myself," she said. "I could sweet talk Hank and maybe get a little more leeway with the college girls."

"Is this dirty old man threatening to the coeds?" I asked. "Because I'd rather be just about anywhere else."

"Maybe," she said. "Let me give it a try."

"It's all yours," I said. "I'll take Red up the mountain tomorrow. You go back without me."

"You did say that I had the lead on this one," she said.

"And I meant it," I replied. "Do your thing. Let me know how it's going."

"Thanks, Breeze," she said. "Most men would feel threatened. They don't like to let a woman assume authority."

"You're better suited," I said. "Doesn't bother me one bit. When we get a case that involves mature adult women, I'm all in."

"No doubt," she said. "Officer Will was a mature adult. You were all over that."

"And the case was solved," I said. "Proving my point."

"We each have our strong points, I suppose."

"I promise not to get in trouble in the woods with Red tomorrow," I said. "Unless he gets hit by a skunk or something."

"If so, he's your dog," she said.

I let the conversation rest at that point. I knew that we'd overcome my weak moments with Angelina Will, but it was clear Brody could bring it up whenever it would help her win an argument. I had to accept that. She deserved that much. Meanwhile, our relationship was better than ever. So much so that I'd finally agreed to get phones and access to the internet. We couldn't run a business without those tools. We didn't need to run a business, but it was something that Brody wanted to do. I'd been involved in all sorts of action since we'd moved to the mountains. She'd been sitting home baking cookies and hoping that I didn't get myself killed. I understood her need to be involved. I'd even encouraged it. That led to opening Creekside Investigations and all that would come with it. We were equal partners, with complementing skill sets.

Brody spent the next few days trolling the campus alone. I used the time to give my dog plenty of exercise and to split wood for the next winter. I was the more productive one. Brody hadn't accomplished much except to ingratiate herself to the head of security. She hoped to be able to move about more freely as a result. Her gut feeling was that there was a girl or two who had some information they hadn't divulged. She just needed to figure out who they were and how to get them to talk. She still hadn't found the mysterious Kate, and Hank wasn't helping.

"You need to find some kind of clerk that has the student's information," I suggested. "How many Kates can there be?"

"Or Katherines, Kathys, Katrinas," she said. "Their data is probably protected."

"Make nice with the admissions officer or a professor," I said. "Someone will point her out."

"Unless the wagons are drawn around her," she said. "It's a small, closed community. They all have to know that she was seeing the boy who killed himself."

"What would motivate the pretty and popular Kate to date a loser like Billy?"

"Love is blind," she replied. "Or so they say."

"Well, I smell a rat," I said. "He never had a girlfriend in high school; then he goes to college and scores a trophy? Just like that?"

"It does seem improbable," she admitted. "But until I'm able to actually talk to someone involved, I've got nothing."

"Something will break soon," I said. "Besides, your badge is holding up well. You've got more time."

A few days later we got a call from the Yancey County Sheriff's Office. Some meth-head had escaped from custody while being transported to court. He'd run off into the woods at the base of Mount Mitchell. He was handcuffed so he should be easy to apprehend, but a hound dog would help in the search. I agreed to make the ninety-minute drive that afternoon. Red was excited to get in the car, knowing that he had a mission.

I'd brought minimal gear, thinking that the job wouldn't take long. A deputy handed me some articles of clothing previously worn by the escapee.

"I'm Dave," he said. "Me and Junior will be following you up the mountain."

"Great," I said. "I don't know the area. This guy's harmless right?"

"Unarmed and handcuffed," he said. "Fast runner though, or the transporting officers would have got him right away."

"He won't outrun Red," I said. "Ready when you are."

We set out at a brisk pace. Red was on the scent instantly and eager to run. I kept him on the leash until we got well away from the road. I was worried that the convict would circle back to the blacktop to try to catch a ride. He couldn't last long on a mountain with hands bound. Once we got high enough, I cut him loose.

"Go get him, boy," I said. "Sniff him out."

He shot off like a rocket and disappeared into the trees.

"Best get a move on," I told the deputies. "Don't want to get too far behind him."

The three of us hustled after the dog. Red wasn't like a coonhound in that he didn't bark and yell the whole time he was tracking. He was all business. If he cornered the man, he'd give me a yelp to let me know. He wouldn't go crazy unless he felt threatened. I figured he could hold his own against an unarmed methhead.

The deputies quickly fell behind. I maintained a brisk pace so that I could spot the dog occasionally. When I lost contact, I called for him. He answered with a single bark to let me know where he was. The officers could see me better than I could see Red, but our line was getting stretched out. There'd been no sign of the escapee yet, so I yelled for Red to stop. I caught up to him, and we waited for the deputies. All of us caught our breath before restarting the chase.

Red barely tolerated our weakness. He wasn't the least bit tired. He was also having a blast. He lived for days like this one. It was how he earned his keep, plus it gave him a sense of pride. He was a damn good pet, and he was a topnotch tracker. I was happy to give him this outlet whenever I got the chance. Red did all the work, and I got all the credit.

It was another hour before things got serious. Red was zeroing in on his target. I made some hand signals to the deputies, trying to tell them to spread out. If the guy was really fast, I didn't want him slipping through us or getting around us. It was more likely that he was tired and hungry. His little brush with freedom would soon come to an end. He'd be happy to get something to eat and a place to sleep.

Red started barking at a patch of thick rhododendrons. Our boy was soon cornered. The three of us surrounded the area Red was pointing out.

"Come on out of there, Mack," Dave said. "Ain't no escaping this time."

A skinny man with black teeth burst out of the weeds and ran like hell. He managed to get between Dave and Junior by pure chance. Red looked at me, eager to run again.

"Go after him, Red," I said. "Go get him."

I watched as my dog quickly closed the distance between him and the runner. He'd never taken down a suspect physically, and I doubted he would now, but I was curious to see what his plan was. I jogged after the two of them with the deputies following behind.

Red caught up to Mr. Black Tooth and ran right by him before turning around. The man zigged left, but Red cut him off. He tried to zag right, but once again Red blocked him. The man tried to kick my dog. He missed, but now I was angry. I sped up and put a shoulder down, hitting the asshole like a linebacker. By the time I got to my feet, the deputies had him.

"We can all walk down this mountain peacefully," Dave said. "Or Junior here can put a lump on your head, and we'll drag your sorry ass down."

"I give up," he said. "Damn dog."

"How'd you think you were going to survive out here numbnuts?" Dave said.

"Guess I didn't think it through," he said.

"Probably why you're in jail in the first place," Dave said. "I've seen smarter warts on a frog."

Black Tooth had no witty reply, so we continued downhill in silence. Halfway down Junior commented that it had been a while since he'd clubbed a convict.

"I'm not encouraging you to try anything mind you," he said. "But it would feel good to crack your skull."

"I got it, I got it," Black Tooth said. "I ain't running no more."

"Maybe you're not as stupid as we thought," Junior said.

That was all there was to it. The rest of the walk was uneventful. After the deputies secured the escapee in a patrol car, they asked for some of my business cards.

"Send an invoice to the Sheriff's Office," Dave said. "If it's too much the Sheriff will let you know."

"Nice working with you," I said. "This is my first trip to Mount Mitchell. Looks like it would be a real bitch in the winter."

"Highest peak east of the Mississippi," Dave said. "Almost seven thousand feet."

"I had a job on Grandfather," I said. "Thought I'd freeze to death."

"That poaching thing?" he asked.

"Yeah, how did you know?"

"The police fraternity is pretty tight-knit," he said. "We have an interest in what our fellow officers are getting into."

"Those poachers were comfortable on the mountain," I said. "But I was able to track them, mostly because they didn't know someone was after them."

"The bad guys aren't often the smartest," he said. "Gives us an advantage."

"Maybe I'll see you guys again," I said. "Put in a good word."

"Will do."

I grabbed a treat out of the glove box and rewarded Red for his efforts. He devoured his doggy bone, leaving a pool of slobber and crumbs at his feet. I rubbed behind his ears vigorously.

"Atta boy, Red," I said. "Good job, boy."

He climbed into the back seat and plopped down for the ride home. I listened to him snoring halfway to Banner Elk. It had been a good day for us as a team. I'd been afraid he'd gotten rusty after a long layoff, but he was as good as ever. He looked happy too.

An Avery County Sheriff's car was running radar just north of Newland. I saw it in plenty of time to make sure I wasn't speeding. As I crawled by I spotted Angelina Will behind the wheel. I reflexively waved to her. She gave her car horn a short honk. I kept an eye on the rearview mirror, hoping she wouldn't follow, or worse, pull me over for old time's sake. Her car didn't move. I was free to continue. Everyone gets a little nervous in the presence of a police car, including me. Our past gave the situation an extra push of paranoia.

I relaxed after that brief encounter and enjoyed the rest of the ride. It was beautiful country, especially in the spring. The rhododendrons were in full bloom, and an assortment of wildflowers had sprung up alongside the roadways. I was proud of myself and Red for a good day's work. I'd made acquaintance with another police agency and left a good reference for Creekside Investigations. It couldn't have gone better.

Brody was beside herself when I got home. She'd learned the identity of the girl who'd been dating Billy Buck, but she had no car to get to the campus. Classes were over for the day. She'd pay the girl a visit tomorrow.

"Her name is Kathrine Leslie," she said. "Freshman from the Charlotte area."

"What have you learned about her so far?"

"No Facebook but she has an Instagram account," she said. "You've got to sign up to see anything. I figured you wouldn't want to do that."

"You figured right," I said. "She's only five miles away."

"I'll find her tomorrow," she said. "See what she's all about."

"Good luck," I said. "Red and I have earned a lay day. We got the bad guy and made some new friends."

"Awesome," she said. "Congratulations. How much you plan to bill on that one?"

"I think a thousand bucks is fair," I said. "You?"

"Might be a little high," I said. "We don't want to scare them off from hiring us again."

"Special introductory offer?"

"I'm thinking five-hundred," she said. "If we get more work from them we'll up it slowly, depending on the time involved."

"It was a pretty easy job," I admitted. "Red did all the work."

Three

I got a surprise when Brody came home from the campus the next day. She was frustrated.

"I hit a brick wall," she said.

"Did you meet the girl?"

"I did, and she was polite but dismissive," she said. "She completely denied ever having dated the kid. She turned up her nose at the thought of it."

"So Billy was lying to his parents?"

"The other girls I spoke to laughed at his name," she said. "They all agreed that Kate would never stoop so low."

"The plot is not thickening," I said. "It's thinning out. But what was his motive for making up a story about dating the hot, popular chick?"

"She was pretty," Brody said. "The girls in her circle are all reasonably attractive too. Seemed smart, upper class."

"And farm boy Billy claims to be dating a real catch, at least to his parents," I said. "We need to find some boys who knew him, his roommate maybe. See just how full of shit he was."

"Might be a job for you," she said. "I can find out who his roomie was. Should have already thought of that."

"We're still feeling our way with this," I said. "I'm happy to help."

Billy's roommate was Pat Grant, an aspiring banker majoring in economics. He went to high school in Charlotte, played sports, and was a member of the honor society. He now had a dorm room to himself, at least temporarily, in the Virginia Residence Hall. It was housing for freshmen men only. I donned my visitor's badge and found his room.

"Knock, knock," I said, pushing open the door that was already ajar.

"Who is it?"

"The name's Breeze," I said. "I'd like to ask you some questions about your former roommate."

"On behalf of whom?" came the reply.

"His parents," I said. "I'm a private investigator."

"Am I obligated to talk to you?" he asked.

"May I come in?"

"Suit yourself," he said.

I extended my hand, but he didn't take it. He did eye my cheap visitor's badge. It didn't exactly scream authority. He didn't offer, but I took a seat anyway.

"You are under no legal obligation to answer my questions," I said. "But refusing to do so will cast doubt on your motives for failing to cooperate."

"He jumped off the top of the spillway," he said. "That's what they said. I wasn't there, and I had nothing to do with it."

"Do you know a girl named Kate?" I asked. "Katherine Leslie?"

He almost winced when I said the name. He looked up and to the left, pausing before answering. He wanted to lie, but it would be easy enough to find out if he knew the girl.

"I know her," he said. "Same circle of friends."

"Did Billy ever tell you that he was dating her?"

I watched him grind his teeth, and I noticed his fingers fidgeting.

"That's ridiculous," he said. "Would never happen."

I continued adding up the physical clues that told me he was lying. The question was why.

"She's out of his league, huh?" I asked.

"Way out, man," he answered. "Where did you hear that he was dating her?"

"His parents," I said. "They said he'd been on two dates with her. That he was happy, that's why he wouldn't kill himself."

"That's a crazy story, mister," he said.

"It's Breeze," I told him. "My name is Breeze, and his parents were sincere."

"Sure they believed their son," he said. "But that doesn't make it true."

"I tell you what, Pat," I said. "There is no punishment for lying to me today, but if this case ever gets to court, you might want to rethink your answers."

"What's that supposed to mean?"

"You're being evasive," I said. "I have no doubt about that. I don't know why, but there it is."

"I'm not lying," he said defiantly. "I don't even have to talk to you."

"But you already have," I said. "And you haven't been telling me the whole truth. I don't know why that is, but there has to be a reason. Maybe you're an accomplice or an accessory after the fact."

"Now you're pissing me off," he said. "Get out."

"No problem," I said. "Have a nice day."

I hesitated before leaving, staring him down. This was his chance to tell me to go fuck myself or get physical. He wisely chose neither course of action. I turned and walked out, leaving the door open. I heard him slam a fist on his desk.

Back at the cabin, I told Brody about my encounter with the young Pat Grant.

"He denied everything," I said. "Just like Kate. He was an arrogant little bastard."

"Why is it that I don't want to believe them?" Brody asked.

"Did you get a sense that Kate was lying to you?"

"She was convincing, but teenage girls excel at it," she said. "Conniving little bitches."

"You were a teenage girl once," I pointed out.

"That's how I know," she said. "I grew up with a bunch of schemers and manipulators."

"What a strange world we live in," I said. "The greatest thing on Earth to a teenage boy is a teenage girl, but the girls have a leg up in the maturity department. Now you tell me they're manipulative too. How's a kid to survive that stage of his life?"

"You seemed to have managed," she said.

"I had the same girlfriend all through high school," I told her. "She wasn't a devious person."

"You think she told her parents about your backseat shenanigans?"

"We were careful," I said. "Her folks trusted me. Neither of us wanted to betray them."

"How fifties," she said.

"It was the seventies," I replied. "They were good people."

"What happened to her?" she asked. "Do you know?"

"Husband and kids in the Tidewater area," I said. "Last I knew, but that was a long time ago."

"You really don't look back do you?"

"Those days are long gone," I said. "Hell, my marriage seems like a century ago now. Time marches on."

"And we live for today," she said. "You taught me that."

"With an eye towards tomorrow," I said. "That's the lesson I learned from you."

"Back to the case," she said. "Kate denies. Pat denies. Friends deny. Have we determined that Billy lied to his parents?"

"Every indication points to yes," I said. "But Pat Grant was hiding something. He's a bad liar."

"I don't think I'll get a second chance to interview those girls," she said. "They were like a pack of hyenas, parroting the same line.

Holding their nose at the thought of Billy Buck getting anywhere near them."

"We need to rethink our approach," I said. "Let's sleep on it and come up with a way to get to the truth."

"I want to talk to his parents again," Brody said. "Look into their eyes. If I believe them we'll have to continue with this."

"I already believe them," I said. "But sure. I'll try to get Frank aside. Have a man to man talk."

"Good," she said. "No point in returning to campus right now. We've ruffled their feathers."

"They'll have more time to coordinate their stories," I said.

"Seems to me they've already done that," she said.

"Someone on that campus knows what happened," I said. "How do we find that person?"

"I don't know," she said. "Short of enrolling in classes."

Brody called Frank and Darla and made arrangements for us to visit the next day.

They were anxious to hear what we'd learned so far. After we parked behind their porch, I went to the barn while Brody went to meet Darla at the back door. I found Frank working on an old tractor that had seen better days.

"Need a hand?" I asked.

"Naw," he said. "I can take this thing apart and put it back together blindfolded."

"What's the problem?"

"Injectors," he said. "I pull them out and try to clean them before I spend the money for new ones."

"That's what I always did on my boat," I told him. "Saved a lot of money over the years."

"A tractor engine is a different animal," he said. "Simple and strong, but still needs care."

"As a matter of fact," I said. "My boat had a Ford Lehman in it. Tractor engine converted for marine use."

"No kidding?" he asked. "Never heard of such a thing."

"They put a heat exchanger on it instead of a radiator," I explained. "Used sea water to cool it."

"Separate water pump for that?"

"Yup," I answered. "It constantly needed a new impeller. Pain in the ass."

"This old girl gets grain and chaff jammed up in the grill," he said. "Causes her to get hot once in a while. I have to stop what I'm doing and clean it all out."

"Probably got a million hours on her though," I said.

"At least," he said. "It will be the last one I ever own if I can help it."

"Tell me about your conversations with Billy about the girl," I said.

"He was excited to tell me about her," he said. "Thought it was the best thing that ever happened to him."

"He thought that, or you thought that?"

"Well, both of us I suppose," he said. "We never made any headway with the boy here on the farm. We weren't gung ho about him going to college either, but we thought maybe it would give him a chance in life that he couldn't get here at home. We stressed over the decision for months. Darla had me get on my knees and pray with her over it. When he brought us the paperwork for Lees-McRae, we felt we had our answer. When he said he had a girlfriend, we knew we'd done the right thing."

Frank's wrench slipped off and he busted a knuckle on the engine. This is where I would have cussed and bitched, but he was stoic. He stepped back calmly and surveyed the damage. His hand was bleeding, and the blood was mixing with grease.

"Let me," I said, picking up the wrench. "You should clean that up."

"Be right back," he said calmly.

I'd pulled the injectors on my old Lehman more times than I could remember. I had the drill down pat. Before he could return from the house, all six injectors were on his workbench, ready to be cleaned. I didn't bust a single knuckle, which was a rare thing. I figured it was because of all the room I had to work in, as opposed to a boat's engine room. I may have even enjoyed the chore.

"I'll be," he said. "You do know your way around a tractor engine."

"Glad to help," I said. "When you and Billy were talking about this girl, did you have any reason to question his story?"

"Billy was proud of himself," he said. "He knew that I'd be proud of him. I remember it as a poignant father-son moment."

"You have zero doubts about it?" I asked. "You're absolutely certain that he was telling the truth?"

"I have no reason to think otherwise," he said. "We're simple folk, Mr. Breeze. The boy never was slick to the ways of the secular world. We still sat at the dinner table and talked each night. He favored his mother, but he came to me first about the girl. It was a bonding experience for us."

Frank Buck believed what he was telling me with all his heart. He was a straightforward man with no reason to attempt to deceive me or anyone else. I believed him. I could also see that he was still hurting, even though he tried his best not to show emotion.

"We found the girl," I said. "Brody talked to her."

"What did she say?"

"She denied ever dating Billy," I said. "Her friends backed up her story."

"Why would she do that?" he asked.

"I can't speak for her," I said. "But maybe she's afraid of being mixed up in his death."

"Maybe she is mixed up in it," he said. "That's probably why she's lying."

"I also spoke to Billy's roommate," I told him. "He knows this Kate. He said there's no way she would ever see Billy."

"Billy didn't like that boy much," he said. "Said he was a stuck-up rich kid."

"He was right about that," I said. "He was not respectful to me. I gave him a chance to come at me, hoping that he would so I could put him in his place."

"Violence is never the answer," he said. "Even when it feels like it would help."

"He didn't take the bait," I said. "Lucky for him."

"We don't want any of that in our name," he said. "We just want to know the truth."

"So far, everyone we've talked to disputes your son's claim," I said. "Personally, I think the roommate is being deceptive. Brody didn't get that from the girl but allows for the possibility. She says teenage girls are notoriously manipulative."

"I met my wife as a teenager," he said. "In church. Thirty years together now."

"That's great," I told him. "You need each other now more than ever."

"If you can find out what happened to our boy," he said. "We'll survive this. Not knowing the truth is furthering our grief, especially Darla. Will you keep digging?"

"Of course we will," I said. "Just know that we're up against it so far."

"I take you for a resourceful man," he said. "You've been in tougher situations. You'll get to the bottom of this."

"You're an astute observer," I said. "But I'm counting on Brody to crack this. I've lost any persuasive skills I ever had with teenage girls."

"Intriguing perspective," he said. "I don't suspect we'd have been friends in our youth."

"I'm a much better man that I used to be, Frank," I said. "Trust me on that."

"Plus you have Brody," he said. "Seems like a good match."

"We're a team," I said. "For better or for worse."

"Get to the truth," he said. "That's all we ask of you."

"Soak those injectors in brake cleaner or something," I said. "Let them sit for a while."

"Here comes your gal," he said.

"We'll go now," I said. "Thank you for your time."

"Thanks for your help," he said. "Likely saved me another knuckle."

Brody and I waved goodbye as we got in the car. Darla and Frank met in the middle of the yard and hugged. I felt bad for them.

"We have got to figure this out," I said. "For their sake."

"I agree," she said. "Darla cried most of the time I was in the house. She's convinced that Billy was telling the truth."

"So is Frank," I said. "I believe them."

"Me too, but how do we proceed?"

"Have you been handing out our business cards to everyone you talk to?" I asked.

"I have," she replied. "You think someone will come forward?"

"We can hope."

"A wise man once told me to shit in one hand and hope in the other, see which one fills up first."

"That was wish in the other," I said.

"Same thing," she said. "I don't like being passive."

"We'll think of something."

Three days went by without either of us thinking of a damn thing. I finally decided to speak with the police chief in Banner Elk. I did not expect a pleasant reception. My history with that department was a mixed bag. I'd worked with them to solve cases, but I'd also caused the downfall of the previous chief. He was a devious bastard that used his position to hurt people and benefit himself. I took it upon myself to not only get him fired but to ruin his reputation permanently. As a result, he tried to kill me, but other officers had taken him down with well-placed bullets. His replacement was suspicious of me, which was only natural.

All of the cops involved knew that I'd been responsible for a sophisticated smear campaign that brought down the old chief.

They just didn't know how I'd been able to accomplish that. Some of them respected me for it. Others were afraid of me. Additionally, my last mission had involved the Beech Mountain Chief of Police. I now had a history of exposing wrongdoing by law enforcement. I also had a track record of helping them solve crimes. In my eyes, only a bad cop would have a problem with me. The good cops would feel that I was an asset to law enforcement.

If the new Chief harbored ill-will towards me, he kept it bottled up. He greeted me professionally and invited me into his office. I watched him closely, trying to get a physical clue as to his feelings about me. He was wary but willing to hear me out.

"Billy Buck," I said. "His parents are convinced that he didn't kill himself."

"As any parent would be," he said.

"Can you bring me up to speed on why that particular determination was made?"

"No clues that anyone else was present," he said. "No witness came forward to say otherwise. Anyone that knew the kid called him a loser. He was having a tough time at school."

"With classes or socializing?"

"He was an outcast," he said. "Widely known and corroborated."

"Did you run a toxicology test?"

"We did," he said. "But we don't have the results yet. Takes four to six weeks."

"So you made the call without it?"

"I don't see how it matters," he said. "Finding drugs in his system would only bolster our findings."

"That depends," I said.

"How?"

"It's my belief that the boy didn't do drugs," I said. "Maybe someone got him to smoke a joint or something harmless like that, but if you found serious shit in his system that could indicate foul play."

"Farmboy from Hickory is not going to drop acid?" he asked.

"No, he wouldn't," I said. "Or smoke crack or any number of other drugs that are probably available on that campus."

"You know it has a religious affiliation, right?"

"Doesn't matter," I said. "It's a college. There are drugs there."

"There is no history of a drug problem at Lees-McRae," he said.

"Did you go to college?" I asked.

"Military," he said.

"Ever see any drugs on base?"

"Of course," he answered.

"Would anyone in the community openly say there was a drug problem on that base?"

"No, they wouldn't," he said. "But it was there."

"See my point?"

"I guess I do," he admitted.

"Did you ever smoke dope?" I asked.

"Couple of times," he said. "When I was young and dumb."

"How about acid?"

"Never," he said. "Never considered harder drugs."

"So if you were found dead and a coroner found acid or meth in your system, what would your parents think?"

"Impossible," he said. "Couldn't happen."

"Someone spiked your drink," I said. "Or injected you against your will."

"The tox results just got more interesting," he said. "I follow. Maybe we should have waited."

"Can you contact me when you get the results?" I said.

"Why should I?"

"You should know that Billy Buck's parents hired me," I said.

"No, I didn't."

"Then you're not paying attention," I said. "We have reason to believe that it was not a suicide. Can't prove it yet, but we're working on it."

"Is this the first case for Creekside Investigations?" he asked.

"You should really get out more," I said. "I helped apprehend an escaped convict just the other day at Mount Mitchell."

"The meth-head?" he asked. "That was you?"

"Me and my dog," I said. "Here, take my card. Call me when you need my help."

He looked at me long and hard, studying me. He put my card in his desk drawer and stood up.

"I still haven't figured you out, Breeze," he said. "You're a good guy, and you're a bad guy. You take down cops, and you take down crooks. What is your deal?"

"I don't take down good cops," I said. "That's all you need to concern yourself with. I can help if you'll accept it. We've got our license. Brody was FBI. We can work together."

"I'm going to ask that you leave the campus alone until we get those drug test results back," he said. "Let's see what they tell us. I'll call you. We can go from there."

"Understood," I said.

Four

Brody was pissed that the Chief wanted us to stay away from the campus. The only way we had to move forward was to talk to the students.

"We can't wait another week or two for those results," she said. "Hank won't let me back by then."

"I thought you'd won him over with your sparkling eyes and enchanting smile," I said.

"I won his grudging tolerance," she said. "Remember those visitor passes? He thinks they'll fall apart."

"The Chief is a higher authority," I pointed out. "We can't afford to be on his bad side. He's suspicious of me as it is."

"This town needs a female chief that you can charm," she said.

"Ha ha, funny girl," I said. "I don't blame him for being wary. I'm responsible for what happened to his predecessor."

"Without which he wouldn't have the job," she said. "You did him a favor."

"That's one way to look at it," I said.

"Try winning him over instead of butting heads," she said.

"Easier said than done," I said. "But I'll look for an opportunity to try."

"You do that," she said. "We need peace with the natives if we want to stay here."

She was right as usual. I'd rubbed the new Chief the wrong way from day one. I didn't like his attitude when we'd originally met. First impressions are sometimes wrong. I had to give him a chance if I wanted the same courtesy. I decided to speak with him again and deliver some kind of peace offering. I drove down to town the very next day.

"You again?" he asked. "Did you lose something here or what?"

"I came to apologize," I said. "We didn't start off on the right foot. I don't blame you for being standoffish. I'd probably do the same."

"First you got the man fired," he said. "Then you got him killed. Why would I trust you?"

"He got himself killed, by other cops who were defending my life," I said. "If those guys thought I was bad news, they could have let him shoot me."

"I was briefed," he said. "Highway Patrol did the right thing. It's the background that concerns me."

"Understandable," I said. "But he was dirty. He needed to go."

"And you took it upon yourself to arrange his departure," he said. "No one can figure out how you managed to do that. A mystery that's caused a lot of speculation."

"I broke no laws," I said.

"I guess I need to know which side you're on," he said. "And if I need to watch my back where you're concerned."

"I'm trying to be on the side of good," I explained. "I can't help who is on the wrong side."

"I'm here to uphold the law," he said. "And to get this department on the right track. I don't need you as a distraction."

"I apologize," I said. "Seriously. My offer of help stands."

"I don't need your services at the moment," he said. "But I'll consider it."

"That's all I can ask," I said, extending my hand.

He took it, and we shook like men. I was grateful that he didn't try to do the macho thing and crush my hand. It was a firm and meaningful gesture. I felt better about our potential relationship as a result.

"Thank you, Chief," I said.

"Now get out of my hair," he said. "If I want to see you again I'll call you."

"Yes, sir," I said.

I drove back home and told Brody about our exchange. She'd been skeptical that I could pull it off. I'd never been the most tactful person. She had explained that I needed to learn when discretion was the better part of valor.

"Was that so hard?" she asked.

"I swallowed my pride and apologized," I said. "He seemed to accept that."

"Good job," she said. "We'll teach you some manners yet."

"Yes, ma'am," I said.

"Now we'll sneak around behind his back and visit the campus."

"Now who is coloring outside the lines?" I asked.

"Billy Buck's death will fade from memory, and the whole episode will blow over," she said. "We've got to strike while memories are fresh and there is still a sense of urgency."

"How do you plan to find the one kid who is willing to talk?" I asked. "Peer pressure is a powerful thing at that age. The word is out to keep quiet."

"A kid like Billy," she suggested. "Someone who overheard a conversation. Some invisible kid that's not in the clique. A kid who would love to spill the beans on the snobs who've mistreated him, or her."

"But that hasn't come forward already," I said. "Afraid maybe. Or maybe no one has asked them."

"Right," she said. "Change our focus from the cool kids to the uncool kids."

"Might work," I said. "Can't be worse than what we've accomplished so far."

"It has to be me," she said. "You've made peace with the Chief. You should stay away from the college."

"Have at it G-man," I said. "I trust your abilities."

It was progress. I'd smoked the peace pipe at the Banner Elk PD, and we'd come up with another line of attack for Lees-McRae College. Our investigation wasn't dead just yet. We'd keep beating the bushes, looking for the truth. If we failed, we could tell ourselves, and Billy's parents, that we'd done our best.

Brody spent the next few days sneaking around the campus. I used the time to send out mailers to the various police agencies in Avery and Watauga Counties promoting Creekside Investigations. We took out small ads in several newspapers as well. Earning a bunch of money wasn't the real goal. If we were going to run a business, we wanted it to be successful. Our overhead was practically zero, and I doubted we could count dog food as a business expense.

I listened each night as Brody replayed the day's events. Randomly talking to strangers wasn't panning out for her. We needed to find a way to target the right students.

"Can you get his class schedule?" I asked.

"The college isn't cooperating," she said. "They don't want me there."

"Ask his mother," I suggested. "Maybe she has a copy or knows what classes he was taking at least."

"Good idea," she said. "I'll call her right now."

I played with Red while she made the call. He was acting more lively since his trip to Mount Mitchell. The mission had done him good. I'd been trying to run him more often and not let him get lazy lying around the house. He was a valuable partner in our business. I wanted him to be ready when I needed him. Every few days I'd take a pair of dirty socks out of the laundry basket. I hid one on our property somewhere, then let him smell the other one. He'd dutifully run off and find the lost sock with glee every time. It was his favorite game.

Darla Buck said she had a copy of Billy's class schedule somewhere and that she'd call back as soon as she found it. It took less than ten minutes for the phone to ring. Freshmen took mostly required subjects, like English 101. Billy's lone elective was computer science. Brody wrote down the professor's name and the location of the class. This would help narrow her search for someone that knew Billy, but was outside the clique she'd been dealing with.

That particular class was held Tuesdays and Thursdays at one in the afternoon. The college had no major or minor program in Computer Science, just that one class. They didn't offer a journalism major either, but they did have a Major in English. Brody went to see what she could do on her own. We decided that a pretty woman would have a better chance of talking to geeks and nerds than a man would.

She hung around outside the computer lab that Tuesday, finding kids that knew Billy. Several admitted to knowing him, but chose not to talk. They were obviously nervous and shy. Any attempt to press them about Billy's death would cause them to clam up immediately. It seemed to be a sore subject on campus, as if every student had been instructed not to talk about it. She handed out our business card to everyone who would take it, hoping that one of them would call us later.

"They know something they're not telling me," she said. "I can feel it. All of them are afraid to tell the truth."

"Do you think the campus administration is responsible?" I asked.

"I don't think that's it," she said. "We were dealing with the popular kids from families with money. The less social kids don't want to be seen as rats. They might not have a chance to join the cool group, but they don't want to be pariahs either."

"Or worse," I said.

"What do you mean?" she asked.

"Let's hypothesize that Kate and her friends somehow caused Billy's death," I began. "Other kids know, but if they squeal, they face physical harm."

"From teenage girls?"

"Boys," I said. "That Pat Grant kid had a mean streak to him. He's the enforcer. There may be more. Jocks who will protect the popular girls."

"Straight out of a movie," she said. "Animal House or Porky's?"

"All fiction is based on fact," I said. "College campuses are closed societies, with a bunch of subgroups. Billy didn't make up a fantasy about Kate to tell his parents, or else we're wasting our time."

"We committed to seeing this through," she said.

"Is it plausible that Kate and company killed Billy somehow?" I asked. "And now they are succeeding at covering it up?"

"Not probable," she said. "But I suppose it's possible."

"What about upperclassmen?" I asked.

"Seniors don't give a shit about what the freshmen are up to," she said. "But why? What's the motive?"

"No idea," I said. "At least not yet. If our boy didn't commit suicide, then somebody killed him. It's an either-or proposition."

"Unless it was an accident," she added.

"He decided to walk out on the spillway and slipped, falling to his death?"

"Or he was goaded," she said. "Drawn into the cool kid's circle as a plaything to be humiliated."

"That does sound possible," I said. "Good brainstorming."

"We still need someone to admit that," she said. "Or someone who witnessed it to come forward."

"There must be one kid on that campus with a conscience."

Several more days went by with no progress down at Lees-McRae. Brody was getting increasingly frustrated. I felt useless. This was a strange turn of events for us, as I'd always been the man on a mission while she stayed behind. Now I was staying home, and she was the lead investigator. It wasn't going well, though that wasn't her fault.

Later that week I got a call from the Banner Elk Police Chief. He asked me to pay him a visit at my earliest convenience. I drove down to town right away.

"Have you ever heard of Rohypnol?" he asked.

"Roofies?"

"Exactly," he said. "It was in Billy Buck's system."

"Somebody Roofied him?"

"Unless he took it himself," the Chief said.

"Doesn't seem likely," I replied. "Christian farm boy. Pretty innocent to the ways of the world. I could see him taking a toke from a joint maybe, but not voluntarily taking a powerful sedative."

"Maybe he didn't know what it would do," he said.

"You know as well as I do how this drug gets into someone's system," I said. "Someone put it in his drink."

"That's generally how it happens, yes," he admitted.

"Are you going to take a new look at his death, now?"

"It's the last thing I wanted to do, but I have no choice," he said. "The college will not be pleased."

"They should want to know the truth," I said.

"Not if it creates negative publicity," he said. "As far as I know, nothing like this has ever happened at that school. They maintain a stellar reputation."

"How far would they go to protect that?" I asked.

"You're not suggesting the administration is covering something up?"

"Someone is," I said. "My first suspects would be the perpetrators."

"Other students," he said.

"Right," I said. "Brody has been working that angle, but she's being stonewalled. Maybe actual law enforcement can get some answers out of those kids."

"Which kids?"

"Katherine or Kate Leslie for starters," I said. "Pat Grant as well. Kate's friends."

"I thought I told you to avoid the campus," he said.

"It's Brody's work, not mine," I said.

He gave me a disapproving look. I explained Billy's story about dating Kate. I told him more about Brody's interview with the students, and my encounter with Pat Grant. He took notes as I spoke.

"I guess you want me to thank you for laying the groundwork," he said. "Even though I asked you to stay away."

"I haven't stepped foot on that campus since you told me not to," I said.

"What do I have to do to keep both of you away?" he asked. "This is suddenly serious police business. I can't have you two interfering."

"We made a promise to the boy's parents," I said. "They knew it wasn't suicide. We believed them enough to look into it. Now the ball's in your court."

"Thanks to you," he said. "I'm not sure if I should appreciate your efforts or not."

"Sorry to make you do some actual police work," I said. "I thought it might liven up your days. Beats writing speeding tickets doesn't it?"

"Lees-McRae is a vital institution in this town," he said. "Putting a blot on their record won't do me any favors."

"Protect and serve," I said. "Justice for all."

"You should read our mission statement," he said. "We are to provide a helpful, visible presence within the community and provide traffic and pedestrian assistance, and a comforting presence. We are merely a watchful eye during both daylight and nighttime hours."

"Are you shitting me?"

"Look it up," he said.

"This particular case calls for a legitimate investigation."

"Which is why I'll call Avery County," he said. "They've got qualified people."

"Deputy Angelina Will," I said. "Chief Investigator. I'm familiar."

"From that Beech Mountain thing, right?"

"Yes, and you've found a way to keep me off campus," I said. "I'd like to steer clear of her if possible."

"It's my lucky day," he said. "I'll ask for her specifically."

"She's a good cop," I said. "That's all you need to know."

"Look, Breeze," he said. "I do appreciate you bringing this to me, but let us handle it from here, okay?"

"Fine, but we need to be kept in the loop to satisfy our obligation to the parents," I said. "If you don't mind."

"Should I have Deputy Will call you?"

"I'd prefer it was you," I said. "Good luck with the case."

That little meeting didn't turn out as I had expected. We were banished from the investigation and Angelina would likely take over, under the Chief's guidance. They had a political tightrope to walk. It was going to be hard to solve a murder on campus without putting a bad mark on the college's record. I didn't envy their task, but I only cared about the truth. My employers were Darla and Frank. I owed my allegiance to them, not to Lees-McRae College.

FIVE

I went home and briefed Brody on my conversation with the Chief. She didn't like being forbidden from visiting the campus. We had a job to do, and she wanted to keep doing it.

"Maybe it's a good thing," I said. "Now that the cops are involved again, maybe the truth will come out."

"Who gives a date rape drug to a teenage boy?" she asked. "That makes no sense at all."

"I don't get it either," I said. "It seems to rule out Kate and friends. Girls don't use Roofies; do they?"

"I would have thought it was strictly male behavior," she said. "Slip it in a girl's drink at a bar or a party."

"Billy's not old enough to drink at a bar," I said. "If he even drank alcohol at all."

"So someone dosed his soda on campus," she said. "How did he end up dead?"

"He was disoriented," I said. "The drug hadn't knocked him out yet, and he walked off the wall at the spillway."

"But why drug him in the first place?" she asked. "Hot girls don't drug nerds so they can screw them. Not that I've ever heard."

"But it's men that would have the drug," I said. "Either a dude drugged him, or he gave the drug to the girls."

"Who could that be?"

"Pat Grant," I said.

"All speculation," she said. "I'd love to put some pressure on those kids."

"We cannot interfere in an active police investigation."

"We can't bill hours for sitting around and waiting. Do you think they can handle it properly?" she asked.

"I'm certain it will be Deputy Will," I told her.

"Your old gal pal Angelina," she said. "She does seem competent. We should fill her in on our thoughts on the matter."

"Call her up," I said.

"I thought we could meet her for coffee," she said.

"I have no pressing need to see her in person," I said. "But if you insist."

I thought I was being clever. I managed to show no interest while agreeing to the visit at the same time. If Brody was laying a trap, I'd sidestepped it adeptly.

"I'm just busting your chops," she said. "I'll give her a call."

I took that opportunity to take Red out back and throw a tennis ball around the yard. Let the women hash it out. I was over it. Angelina was history, and we couldn't cross paths with law enforcement on campus. I saw no alternative but to sit back and let them do their job.

Brody joined us ten minutes later. She had a curious look on her face. She was mulling over something in her mind.

"What's going on?" I asked.

"We had a nice chat," she answered. "But then things got cryptic."

"What do you mean?"

"She said we're about to be offered a job," she replied. "And that we should take it."

"What kind of a job?"

"Something to keep us out of their way. That's all she would say."

"And she advised that we accept? I asked.

"She was quite clear about that," she said. "Like it was important. Not for the job itself, but for our working relationship with the police."

"We can expect some busywork bullshit mission, then," I suggested. "I won't jump at it. I'll ask what it pays first."

"We know it's a game," she said. "They know it too. I don't think we need to play it coy."

We found out the next day when the Avery County Sheriff called. It was about the abandoned hospital on the outskirts of Banner Elk. Cannon Memorial had sat empty for twenty years. It was heavily vandalized and the source of hundreds of rumors concerning paranormal activity. This reputation was spread mostly by college kids. Old-timers recalled the place fondly. Many of them had been born there or visited family members over the years. Assorted ghost hunting groups had elevated the local gossip into full-blown legendary tales of evil spirits. The crumbling remains of the hospital had been featured on more than one television show and hundreds of Youtube videos.

The Sheriff had an idea to curtail the vandalism and late-night visits by students, not just from Lees-McRae, but also from Appalachian State down in Boone. He wanted to make a bunch of arrests and publicize them widely. He'd crack down hard and create a deterrent to future trespassers.

"Where do we come in?" I asked.

"I need someone to stay on the premises overnight for a week or so," he said. "Like a security guard. Just call us if anyone approaches. I can't spare the man-hours to babysit that hellhole."

"Hundred bucks an hour," I said. "I'll give you a week."

"Might take two weeks," he said. "I'll need several arrests. You never know when the vandals will show up."

"Hundred-fifty then," I said. "That's a lot of time away from home, and we could be doing other business."

"Deal," he said. "But aren't you afraid of the spooks?"

"I don't believe in spooks," I said.

"This might change your mind," he said. "Don't park on the premises. You can use the little dirt lot over by the millpond. Go in after dark and stay concealed. The trespassers will come to you."

"I want someone to show up quickly when I call," I said. "We don't want any trouble out of this."

"A deputy will be in the area, and Banner Elk will back us up if necessary."

"When do we start?" I asked.

"Tonight if possible," he replied. "Good luck."

Brody did a little internet research on Cannon Memorial Hospital. There were message boards full of tales of close encounters of the paranormal kind. There were others debunking these claims. None of the videos we watched showed us any proof of ghost or evil spirits. They were all filmed in the dark with poor lighting. The Ghost Hunters Show used some type of electronic equipment to measure activity on some ambiguous frequency. The actors overplayed their roles dramatically. It all looked like a hoax to me. Brody agreed.

"This is nonsense," she said. "Let's load up some supplies and get ready."

We ate a nice dinner, and I took Red for an extended walk before departing for the hospital. We pulled into the millpond parking area just after dark. We waited for traffic to clear and hustled across the road to enter the vacant building. The interior was a mess of decaying ceiling tiles, exposed wires and plumbing, and lots of graffiti. Old medical files were scattered across the floor in one room. Windows were mostly busted out. Doors hung cockeyed on their hinges.

We set up camp in what may have been the lobby. It was the only room that was more or less clear of debris. When we turned off our flashlights, darkness enveloped us completely.

"I have to admit it," Brody whispered. "This is a little spooky."

"Put your light on dim and leave it down low," I suggested. "At least we'll be able to see each other."

"Did we pack extra batteries?"

"One set of spares for each flashlight," I said.

"Just like a Boy Scout," she said.

"Get comfortable," I told her. "This is going to be a long, boring night."

Sometime around midnight, we heard a thud from one of the floors above us. It got our attention. We sat upright and motionless, listening. There were no more noises.

"Probably just a falling ceiling tile," I whispered.

Two more hours passed. I was just about asleep when we heard a second thud. The noise startled me awake.

"Crap," I said.

"What?"

"We're going to have to check it out," I said.

"Like hell we are," she responded.

"What are the odds that two tiles fall on the same night?" I asked. "Maybe some kids came in a different entrance. That's what we're here for."

"Shit," she said.

We were creeping around like cat burglars, trying to be quiet. It was a difficult task due to all the broken glass and tile scattered about. We climbed the south stairwell and entered the hallway on the second floor. We stood still and listened for more noises, but heard nothing. It was so quiet I could almost hear my heart beating. I could definitely feel it. We waited there for fifteen minutes, hearing nothing.

"Nobody's here," Brody whispered. "Let's go back downstairs."

My flashlight blinked out, and the hair on my neck stood up. I gave it a few whacks, but it refused to come back on. The batteries had been fresh, and I hadn't used it much. Normally, I didn't believe in coincidence, but I had to chalk its failure up to something other than evil spirits. As we descended the stairs using Brody's light, mine came back on by itself. I was glad it was working again, but its unexplained failure gave me pause. *Snap out of it, Breeze. There's no such thing as ghosts.*

Brody let out a big sigh when we got back to the lobby. We made ourselves comfortable again, sitting in the dark, waiting for intruders who never came. We called it quits when the first rays of light cleared the mountains. I was dying for a coffee, and a nap was in my near future, but first I had to tend to Red. He cocked his leg on one side of a bush while I used the other side. He wanted to play, but I wasn't up to it.

Brody had the coffee going when I went back inside. She asked if I wanted breakfast, but I declined. Food would have to wait. I called the Sheriff and reported no activity during the night.

"Anything scary happen?" he asked.

"We heard some noises, but it was nothing," I told him.

"Keep track of your hours," he advised. "The County will pay you when this is done."

"What's happening at the college?" I asked.

"Deputy Will is there today," he said. "Your Chief will keep you posted."

We both slept for hours, wasting most of the day. I threw a bunch of extra batteries in my pack and switched out the defective flashlight with a new one. We had bottled water and snacks, plus a light blanket. We'd survived the first night without being attacked or going crazy. There was no reason we couldn't do it for another two weeks. We had some action on the second night.

Four drunk teenagers approached the hospital. They'd emerged from the Christmas tree farm next door, making a lot of noise. One of the boys threw a beer bottle against the concrete, smashing it. Brody was on the phone before they could get inside. They just stepped foot into the lobby when a Deputy's patrol car pulled up. The girls froze. The boys took off running. I didn't think it was a particularly chivalrous thing to do, but that's kids these days.

"Hold them here," I said to Brody. "I'm going after them."

The Deputy was on their heels when the two boys split up. They were younger and likely faster than me, but I didn't have a belly full of beer. The Deputy sprinted between a row of firs, in hot pursuit of the taller kid. The shorter one hung a left before entering the trees. I followed him as best I could until I realized he wasn't running. He'd run out of gas and was now trying to hide. It wasn't a good plan. I stopped and got control of my breathing, slowing everything down. I knelt and concentrated on the sounds of the night. I could hear the Elk River running over the rocks and into the millpond. A car went by on Tynecastle Highway.

I heard him breathing, panting really. He was a few rows over and not far away. I rose to a crouch and planted each step carefully, silently closing in on the boy. There was barely any light, but my eyes were adjusted. I slid through the trees like the imaginary ghosts in the hospital. I spotted the kid, but he didn't know I was there. I gave up sneaking and sprinted the last ten yards, pouncing on him and pinning him to the ground.

"Do as I say and you won't get hurt," I told him, twisting one arm behind his back.

"Okay, okay," he said. "I give up."

I marched him out of the trees and towards the patrol car. The Deputy came soon after, pushing his trespasser in front of him, daring him to run again. Brody came out of the building with the two girls. All four of them were loaded into the back seat. A few minutes before, they'd been laughing and having a good time. Now they were headed to the police station for booking. If they were over eighteen, their pictures would be all over the place the next day. Their parents would be embarrassed. They wouldn't get any leniency either. That was part of the Sheriff's plan. They'd get the maximum punishment allowed by law, to set an example for others.

We spent the rest of the night huddled together in the lobby, dozing in and out of consciousness. No more teenagers came to visit. Back at the cabin, we skipped the coffee and went straight to bed. Our sleep was interrupted by a call from the Sheriff.

"We're not going to announce the arrests just yet," he said.

"Why not?"

"Let's rack up two or three more before we go big with it," he said. "The papers and radio stations are on board."

"No rest for the weary," I said.

"Good work."

During the following twelve days, three more arrests were made. One night the interlopers had escaped, but the Sheriff had enough ammo to launch his anti-trespassing promotion. We didn't hear any more strange noises or see anything remotely paranormal during those two weeks. Consider the haunting story debunked. We watched a featured news story on the Charlotte station one night. Pictures of the offenders were shown, and there was a discussion with the Sheriff himself. The message was loud and clear. Stay away from Cannon Hospital or face harsh consequences. A similar story ran on the Bristol stations. The local newspapers ran their stories too. Fliers were plastered across two college campuses. The campaign was in full swing, and we were off the hook.

When I figured up our bill for the county, I was stunned. Ten hours per night times one-hundred and fifty dollars came to twenty-one thousand for fourteen nights work. I knew that Avery County would shit a brick if I charged them that total, even though the Sheriff had agreed. I wrote up an invoice for ten grand instead. A check arrived one week later. I don't know if the Sheriff ever did the math, but I was hoping that I'd earned some goodwill with him.

We celebrated our windfall over prime rib at Stonewalls. It had become our special occasion destination. I liked the place, but the seven dollar beers kept me from visiting too often. They did a great job with the meat and usually had some enticing specials. We sat by the open fire pit after dinner, watching other diners come and go. Everything was right with our world, except for the death of Billy Buck. We hadn't heard one word from the Chief or Angelina. They'd been back on the case for three weeks. Something should have broken by now.

I let it rest one more day before calling the Chief. He owed me a progress report at least.

"It's been awfully quiet down there in Banner Elk," I said. "What gives?"

"We've done everything but torture those kids," the Chief said. "They stick to their story, which is they know nothing about it. We haven't found the slightest crack."

"Someone on that campus knows the truth," I said. "He didn't die in a vacuum."

"Sure seems that way," he said. "We think he got dosed accidentally. Drank something intended for someone else. Wandered around and took his fall."

"The only people who would have a harder time believing that than me are his parents."

"It wouldn't be a suicide," he said. "If that helps."

"I don't know," I said. "It would be a very small consolation. I'm not buying it."

"We haven't closed the book on this yet," he said. "But it looks like an unfortunate accident."

"Wouldn't you like to know who put Rohypnol in someone's drink? Regardless of who it was intended for?"

"Of course," he replied. "That can't be allowed in our community."

"It's a crime, right?" I asked. "Even if no one dies."

"Infliction of bodily harm, gross negligence," he said.

"What if the wrong person drinks it instead of the intended victim?"

"Plain negligence," he said. "Even if there was no intent it still inflicted harm."

"So you have someone to prosecute," I said. "You just need to figure out who. Besides, this particular case of negligence resulted in death. Got to be more charges for that."

"We can't charge someone with murder if there was no intent," he said. "Billy drank the wrong drink, or our perpetrator spiked the wrong glass."

"If you can't get to the bottom of this, Brody and I will," I threatened. "You've had ample time, and we've cooperated every step of the way."

"Take it up with Deputy Will," he said. "I'm just an observer."

"I was afraid you were going to say that."

"I like her, Breeze," he said. "We work well together, but she's not quite mean enough if you know what I mean. I want to put those kids in a dark room and beat the truth out of them."

"Me too," I said. "But we both know that's not going to happen."

"I've got a proposition for you," he said. "Just between you and me."

"I'm listening."

"Go back to campus," he said. "With my blessing. Both of you. Solve this mess but hand it to me."

"I can see where that would solidify your standing in town," I said. "But it would undermine Miss Will."

"I don't care if the three of you work together," he said. "Just let me handle the finale. Take a little credit."

"Personally, I don't have a problem with that," I said. "But I'll have to run it by Brody, and probably Angelina too."

"See what you can do," he said. "I'd appreciate it."

Six

Our new Chief had no idea how to get those kids to talk, and Angelina had gotten nowhere. In a desperate move, the Chief authorized Brody and me to go back to campus, but only if he could take the credit. I had several questions. Was this arrangement acceptable to us? Could we solve the case? Would Angelina play along? I was going to have to defer to Brody's judgment on this one. She was the real investigator.

"Creekside Investigations has to be recognized," she said. "We didn't start this business to inflate the Chief's ego."

"Good point," I admitted. "What about Angelina?"

"If she had resolved the matter herself, I'm sure she wouldn't want someone else to take the credit."

"But she hasn't," I said. "The question remains, how do we resolve it?"

"Before we got kicked off campus," she said. "We talked about finding someone outside the clique. Someone that knew Billy and might know more."

"Geeks and nerds," I said.

"Right," she said. "Chess club kids, little dorky rocket scientists, whatever."

"Is there an RA in that dorm he lived in?"

"Probably," she said. "Why?"

"It's their job to know what their charges are up to," I explained. "Maybe Billy's RA knows something about him that we don't. What kids he hung out with."

"It's an all-male dorm," she said. "Maybe I can flirt my way to some information."

"You go, girl," I said. "I'll be the quiet muscle in the background, in case you need rescuing."

"I'll find out who to talk to and what room they're in," she said. "Then we make a move."

"What about Angelina?"

"You call her," she said. "Let her know we're back on the case. When we get the goods, we let the Chief know that he has to mention us in his press conference."

"Sounds good," I said. "Let's do it."

The Resident Assistant's name was Mike Rampmeyer. He greeted us in a friendly and open manner. He was incredibly nice and accommodating, unlike the other students we'd talked to. He was a senior, and his position was voluntary, but he got free room and board plus a small stipend. He not only knew everyone in the dorm; he knew their problems. He'd talked to Billy early on.

"Billy was really out of place when he got here," he said. "He had no self-confidence, and the other students didn't make his life any easier."

"How did you advise him?" Brody asked.

"I introduced him to some other students, outside of this dorm," he said. "Kids like him."

"Was he able to make friends?" she asked.

"He joined a book club they were in," he said. "They meet at the Book Exchange a couple of times a week. He practically lived there during his off hours. He only came back here to sleep as far as I could see."

"We'll check it out," I said. "Now what about the cool kids?" Kate Leslie, Pat Grant and the rest."

"What about them?"

"Any connection to Billy?" Brody asked.

He paused too long before answering. The question caught him off-guard. He rearranged some items on his desk.

"I'd like to help you," he said. "But I don't know about any connection. He would never fit in with that group."

"We have reason to believe that he was in contact with them," Brody said. "You know more about it. Why won't you tell us?"

"They spoke poorly of him behind his back," he said. "I don't know what happened between them. I swear."

"Did Kate specifically talk bad about Billy?" she asked.

"Yes," he said. "All of them did. They had no mercy."

"Now he's dead," she said. "They have no shame either."

"Why do you say that?" he asked.

"We think they had something to do with his death," she said. "They're doing a good job of acting like it never happened."

"Why would they kill Billy?" he asked.

"I didn't say they did," she said. "But they had something to do with it. Somebody drugged him."

"How do you know he didn't take the drugs himself?"

"He was Roofied," she said. "Nobody Roofies themselves."

"I didn't know," he said. "This dorm is my area of responsibility. When I'm not in class, I'm here. I don't know a lot about what goes on elsewhere unless someone tells me."

"Do you talk to Pat Grant much," she asked.

"Hardly ever," he said. "He doesn't need my assistance."

"There's got to be some scuttlebutt about Billy and that group," she said. "You would have heard something. It's your job to know."

"I wish I could help," he said. "Like I told you. But I just don't know."

"I think you're lying," I said. "That won't play well when the heat comes down. I realize you want to protect your fellow students, but you don't want Billy's death on your hands."

"I had nothing to do with it," he said.

"You're covering up for the people who did," Brody said. "When the cover-up falls apart, being the resident assistant who took part in it won't look good on your resume."

"If you're hoping that the clock runs out before you graduate, don't," I said. "We'll have this wrapped up soon, with or without your help. You're going to want to be on the side of the good guys."

"I'll try to find out what happened," he said, looking down at his shoes.

"We're going to send a police officer to talk to you next," Brody said. "Maybe you can be honest with her."

I saw the fear in his eyes. He found himself in a place he didn't want to be. He was nice to all the students, popular or not. The cool kids were left standing, and the uncool kid was gone. He knew but wasn't ready to tell. He'd managed to fend off private investigators, but when a real cop put her badge in his face, he might break. It was time to call Angelina.

We met the good deputy at Dunn's Deli, across the street from the Book Exchange.

"What do you have?" she asked.

"A couple of things," I said. "The Chief is letting us snoop around on one condition, that he gets the credit. Brody and I don't care, as long as our fledgling agency gets a mention. We're about to go over there to the Book Exchange, which is where Billy Buck spent his free time. I'll let Brody fill you in on the RA."

"Mike Rampmeyer," Brody said. "Room 310. Nice kid. Serious about his position."

"What does he know?" Angelina asked.

"He knows but he isn't telling us," Brody answered. "We thought you might rattle his chain."

"The private investigators need a real cop to add some gravitas to the situation?" Angelina asked.

"Exactly, which puts you on track to get to the truth," Brody said. "Which the Chief wants credit for."

"What a tangled web we weave," Angelina said. "What do you two want out of this?"

"The truth," I said. "We don't care who gets the credit. What about you?"

"I most certainly would want to get the credit if I solved the case," she said. "This thing is going to be big. Historic actually, but I wouldn't have a case without the two of you."

"None of us has a case just yet," Brody added. "We're willing to work it together with you, but we're not sure how you feel about the Chief using it to boost his career."

"I think the three of us should confront him," Angelina said. "Come up with a way to make all of us happy in the end."

"The task force headed by the Banner Elk Chief of Police, with the assistance of Creekside Investigations and Avery County Deputy Angelina Will, has solved the mystery of Billy Buck's death," I said.

"That will sound a lot better after we figure out how he died," Angelina said. "Or who killed him."

"First things first," Brody said. "But I can go with that."

"I'll go talk to this Rampmeyer fellow," she said. "You two go to the Book Exchange. Let's meet back here in one hour."

I would have never thought that Brody and I would be working in close cooperation with Angelina Will, but I was familiar with odd turns of fate in life. Brody seemed to roll with this new development just fine. We all had the same goal in mind: solve the case, put it to rest and move on. Angelina was a good person and a good cop. She'd been able to put her personal feelings aside in pursuit of the truth. I had to give her credit for that. Brody was the best person I knew and had been a fine investigator in the past. She hadn't let petty jealousy bother her. She wanted to solve the case, first and foremost. For my part, I'd managed to get the two smart people in my life together in a common cause. I was the least useful tool in our box on this one, but I didn't mind. I had two attractive, intelligent women to watch. Maybe I could learn something. If not, the view was nice.

We saw the dorks as soon as we entered the Book Exchange. Three of them sat at a round table with four chairs. I wondered if the empty chair was once Billy's. They each had their nose in a book. They paid us no attention when we walked in. Their books were all old science fiction. I saw Asimov, Heinlein, and Bradbury. It was the type of stuff I read when I was a kid. I thought I might be able to engage them in conversation. I waved Brody off and took a seat in the empty chair.

"I love that stuff you're reading," I said. "Mind if I sit in?"

"What are the three laws of robotics?" Geek number one said.

"A robot may not injure a human being or, through his inaction allow a human to come to harm," I said. "A robot must obey orders given to it by humans except where such orders would conflict with the First Law. A robot must protect its own existence as long as such protection does not conflict with the First or Second Law."

"Almost word for word," Geek number two said. "Impressive."

"Asimov was my favorite," I said. "The movie, not so much."

"Totally agree," Geek number three said. Geeks one and two nodded in the affirmative.

"You don't look like a sci-fi kind of guy," Geek one said.

"I was when the greats were writing," I said. "These days it's all crap. I don't follow it anymore."

We went on to have a long discussion about the Golden Age of science fiction. Back then, the truly great writers of the time came from that field. Big ideas that would later become a reality were the norm. We did indeed land on the moon. Grocery store doors opened magically. Jet packs existed, allowing a man to fly. It was a wonderful time that had long since passed, but here in that book store sat three teenagers reading the classics. I had more in common with these three than with Kate Leslie and Pat Grant. I was never a geek. I had girlfriends and played sports, but this was the stuff that I read back then. I had broken the ice and was welcomed at the table.

As soon as I realized that, I got to the point. "Did you guys know Billy Buck?" I asked.

"You're in his chair," Geek two said. "We've been leaving it open in his honor."

"Should I move?"

"You knew the three laws," he said. "I think it's okay."

"His parents hired us to find out what happened to him," I said. "I was hoping you could help."

"The cops said it was a suicide," Geek three said.

"Do you believe that?" I asked. "You knew him pretty well, right?"

The three of them looked at each other, trying to decide if they should continue this talk. I put my hands up, palms out.

"Don't answer anything you don't want to," I said. "Let me know if I'm making you uncomfortable."

"Is that your wife?" Geek one said, pointing to Brody.

"You could say that," I said. "We've been together a long time."

"She's very pretty," he said. "You're not like us, are you?"

"I read all three of the books your holding," I said. "Plus all the other books by those authors."

"Did you go to college?"

"Frostburg State," I said. "In Western Maryland."

"That's in the mountains too, right?"

"Very much like this," I said. "But with more bars."

"We don't go to bars," he said. "Is that when you read the classics?"

"I read those before I got to college."

"What were you reading then?" he asked.

"I recall The Stand, by Stephen King," I said. "And Dean Koontz. It was a phase."

"What about now?" Geek two asked.

"Black Ops stuff," I said. "Vince Flynn, Wayne Stinnett. Anything Florida related, like Tim Dorsey or Carl Hiassen."

"Not familiar," he said. "But your taste has changed."

"Yours will too," I told him. "But you're laying a good foundation with these books."

"Why are you asking about Billy?" Geek one asked.

"His parents are paying me to find out what happened," I said. "They don't believe it was a suicide."

They all looked at each other again, silently communicating something.

"What do you think?" I asked.

"We've discussed this at great length," Geek one said. "It is our consensus that something else happened. He didn't kill himself."

"What's the basis of your conclusion?" I asked. "And what is your alternative theory?"

"Billy got mixed up with a different crowd somehow," he said. "He didn't belong there, and it went bad for him."

"We don't know exactly what happened," Geek two said. "But those people caused his demise somehow."

"What people?" I asked.

"Kate Leslie and friends," Geek three said. "They're awful people."

"What was Billy doing with them?" I asked.

"He told us he had a date with her," Geek one answered. "He didn't show up here that night."

"And you believed him?"

"We did not," he said. "But when he didn't show up here, we started to wonder."

"Then he told us he was seeing her again," Geek two said. "He didn't come in here that night either."

"So he claimed to go on two dates with Kate?" I asked.

"That was his claim," Geek three said. "We didn't know what to think."

"Did you see him again after the second date?" I asked.

The three nerdy amigos of the book club exchanged glances and shrugs. They fiddled with books and pens. No one wanted to be the first to speak. I moved a little closer to Geek one and spoke directly to him.

"Was the second date the night he got killed?" I asked.

He nodded in the affirmative but didn't speak. I looked at the other two.

"Is that right?" I asked. "He died the night he told you he had a date with Kate?"

They both nodded yes.

"Why haven't you come forward with this information?" I asked. "The police have been all over this campus."

"No one asked us any questions until now," Geek one said. "Besides, we weren't there. We don't know what happened that night."

"It puts Billy with Kate that night," I said. "Pretty important don't you think?"

"He claimed to have a date," he said. "We didn't necessarily believe him."

"Did he joke a lot?" I asked. "Play tricks like that on you guys?"

"No," he said. "But have you seen Kate?"

"What would she be doing with a boy like Billy?" asked Brody.

"Exactly," he said. "Have you asked her?"

"She denies everything," Brody said. "Her friends back her up."

"So what do you want from us?"

"Thanks for telling us what you know," she said. "There is a female police officer on campus who might have some questions for you. Cooperate with her too, okay?"

"We can't tell her any more than we've already said," he said. "We don't know anything else."

We gave each of them our business card and walked back across the street to Dunn's Deli. Angelina arrived a few minutes later. We ordered coffee and sat in a booth near the back.

"Did you get anywhere with the RA?" Brody asked.

"He's a genuinely nice kid," she said. "He's already put out some feelers, trying to determine what went down."

"Anything new?" Brody asked.

"There was a bit of a party that night," she said. "Not in Kate's room, but at Pat Grant's."

"Girls were there?" I asked.

"Yes, all the girls in question, plus Grant and a few other boys."

"Billy Buck?"

"No one would confirm that," she said. "But the RA thinks that he was probably there."

"A third party thinker won't fly in court," Brody said. "We need someone who was there to place Billy in attendance."

"I'm going to question all of them again," she said. "I'm going to bring back a burly, mean-looking deputy to stand over my shoulder."

"Maybe the extra pressure will cause one of them to crack," Brody said. "Have you considered taking them all in and tossing them into a holding cell?"

"I need at least vague probable cause," she said. "I hope to get that soon. Then we split them up and sweat it out of them."

"I like it," I said. "Wish we could watch."

"You know that you can't," she said. "But I'll let you know how it goes. First I've got to rattle one of them into admitting something."

"Good luck," Brody and I said simultaneously.

Progress was excruciatingly slow, but we hadn't come to a full stop. Tiny steps forward were leading us somewhere. We could only keep going. The truth was out there.

Seven

Brody and I were not invited to the upcoming interrogation. We'd run out of other ways to be helpful in the investigation. We reported what little we'd learned to Frank and Darla Buck, who urged us not to give up. While we were waiting for results from Angelina, we got a call from the Watauga County Sheriff's Department.

"We've had several reports of strange activity in a wilderness area," The Sheriff said. "I was wondering if you could poke around and see if anything's going on that we need to know about."

"Like what?" I asked.

"Could be a meth cooking operation," he said. "We've heard enough chatter to look into it."

"Where?"

"On the other side of the Watauga River from the park in Valle Crucis," he said. "Between Homestead Drive and Valley Cay. It's heavily wooded but close to residential areas."

"What sort of suspicious activity?"

"Loser looking dudes carrying propane tanks," he said. "Black tooth vagrants coming out of the woods. Stuff like that."

"Your men can't go in?"

"It's serious bush," he said. "But we're not even sure it's a problem. Just check it out and report back."

"My dog could find them in a day if he could get a whiff of some meth," I told him. "Save us all time and effort."

"I can arrange that," he said. "When can you start?"

"Tomorrow if you want."

"Meet us at the park at ten," he said. "You'll have to forge the river, but it's only a foot or two deep."

"See you then, Sheriff," I said.

Brody went back to Banner Elk while I took on the side job. Red was raring to go when I opened the car door for him. He could tell when he had a job, and he was happy for it. It was a six-mile, downhill drive to the park at Valle Crucis. It was behind the Mast Store Annex and a popular spot for locals and trout fishermen. It was not manned by any sort of park personnel. I could easily envision some meth cookers transporting material through the park to the other side of the river. Only bystanders could see them and these days most folks wouldn't make a simple phone call to rat them out. Except, in this case, some people did. The meth-heads had been too obvious, or too frequent to avoid suspicion.

I parked the car and let Red out to run around for a few minutes. The Sheriff waived my two-dollar fee and ignored my violation of the leash rule. He produced a baggie of crystals.

"This won't hurt him will it?" I asked.

"Just let him smell it," he said. "Don't let him lick it."

"Come here, boy," I called.

Red dutifully came running. I knelt and presented him with the baggie.

"Sniff it, Red," I instructed.

He knew that this was the scent he would need to track. He sniffed cautiously, sensing danger. I asked the Sheriff to come with us down to the riverbank, where I gave Red a second sniff. We waded across the shallowest part of the river to the other side.

"Sniff them out, boy," I said. "Find them."

I waved to the Sheriff while Red worked back and forth along the river's edge. Within a few minutes, he was on the scent.

"Call you later," I yelled to the Sheriff.

Off we went into the woods. Red had no doubt. He was confident in his ability and seemed to urge me to hurry after him. I used my arms to block low tree branches and tried to keep up. This job would be over in no time. Then Red stopped. I was glad for the opportunity to catch my breath. He sniffed off to the west for thirty yards and returned. He followed a scent to the east before coming back to me. He sat at my feet and looked at me.

"What is it, boy?"

He yelped twice and remained sitting at my feet. I wished he could talk. He had something to tell me. He barked twice again, getting up and circling the area. He looked east, then west, and barked twice again. I wasn't sure, but I thought that he had two scent trails. Which one to follow? I motioned to the east, and he took off, still confident. I followed for twenty minutes until we came upon the camp. No one was home. There was a propane burner and several small tanks scattered about. Torn plastic bags littered the ground. The place smelled like ammonia and propane. The ground around the burner was beaten down with heavy use. A pile of empty Pseudoephedrine packs, ammonia bottles, acetone cans, and paint thinner made an ugly mess of the landscape. I couldn't imagine anyone wanting to ingest such a concoction of toxicity.

I put the leash on Red to keep him out of the dangerous trash. The residual vapors made it hard to breathe. I got him out of there and on the trail back. When we came to the previous fork, he wanted to follow the western-leading scent. I let him do his thing, and we found a second site not too far away. Here we found containers labeled "Acid" and "Iodine." I assumed that the meth chefs had decided that it wasn't safe to store these with the propane and ammonia at the other site. No one was there at that time, but it was obvious that the Sheriff's concerns were accurate. Red and I had located the outdoor meth lab.

I tried to call the Sheriff, but my fancy new phone had no signal. I was down in a valley and surrounded by mountains. I wouldn't be able to get through until I got back to the park. I kept Red on the leash on the way back. He was a great tracker and a very obedient dog, but he was prone to run off after squirrels and rabbits. I didn't want to waste time chasing him through the underbrush. Halfway back I heard someone coming. Instead of hiding and observing, I just kept on walking, eventually confronting a sickly looking man on the trail. His teeth were black and what hair he had left was thin. His skin was white as a ghost, hanging off his emaciated frame.

"What are you doing out here, mister?" he asked.

"Just hiking with my dog," I said. "No need for concern."

"People don't hike here," he said.

"My first time," I told him. "The undergrowth is a little thick for my taste. Heading back now."

Red growled, low and long. This character was the source of the scent he'd been following. Everyone knows that dogs are good judges of character. Red was exceptionally well-behaved, and had never growled at any person before. I was alerted to the man's bad intentions. He came at me quick, but without much force. He'd seriously underestimated my ability to defend myself.

I sidestepped his bull-rush and popped him on the back of the head as he went by. It wasn't a solid blow, but he went down anyway. I didn't let him get up. I put a knee in his back and twisted one arm behind his back at an impossible angle. He screamed in pain but I didn't ease the pressure. He kicked and squirmed but couldn't get at me.

"A man and his dog walking peacefully in the woods," I said. "Attacked by a maniac on meth. You made a poor choice, my friend."

"You're breaking my arm," he whined.

"I should crack your skull," I told him. "What the fuck is wrong with you?"

"You're gonna call the cops about what you seen," he said. "I panicked."

"The cops sent me here to find your little lab," I said. "I will be calling them shortly. What to do with you in the meantime is the question."

"Just let me go," he begged. "I'll run off, and you won't ever see me again."

"I wish I could do that," I said. "But you've disturbed my gentle sensibilities with an unprovoked attack. I think you ought to go to jail."

"I won't come at you again," he said. "I made a mistake. If you let me go, you won't have any more trouble out of me."

"I'm afraid it's too late for that," I said.

I had a stout hunting knife strapped to my thigh. The handle was heavy and thick. I used it to give his head a solid thump. This triggered his nap mode. He lay limp on the dirt at my feet.

"Sleep tight, asshole," I said. "Come on, Red. Let's go."

I hurried back to the park and called the Sheriff.

"I found it," I said. "It's broken up into two locations. If you get someone here fast, you can nab one of the architects."

"You've taken someone into custody?"

"No," I said. "Just knocked him out in self-defense. Come grab him before he wakes up."

"On the way."

I waited for the deputies to arrive, then led them to the fallen meth-head. One cop cuffed him and slapped him awake. The other followed me to the cooking site. He took pictures and poked around before asking me to lead him back. The first deputy had the perp in the back of the car when we made it to the park. The Sheriff pulled up and conferred with his deputies before coming over to me.

"Nice work," he said. "Except for the knot on that fellow's head."

"He came at me," I said. "I had no choice. I should claim hazardous duty pay."

"We'll talk more about that later," he said. "Send us a reasonable bill."

"Will do, Sheriff," I said. "Call me anytime."

"What's the latest at Lees-McRae?" he asked.

"We're working with Deputy Will from Avery County," I said. "We've got suspects but no proof yet."

"Suspects?"

"It's a long story," I said. "The Banner Elk Chief is on it. Ask him."

"Is he running the investigation?"

"He's our supervisor," I said. "For what it's worth."

I didn't know the Sheriff that well. I wanted him to call us with jobs, but I wasn't familiar enough to divulge any of the inner workings of our deal with the Banner Elk Police Chief. He was fishing for information that I wasn't willing to give. Choosing favorites among the police fraternity didn't seem like a good idea. I'd made some friends, but I'd also made some enemies. I needed them all to make our business a success. He'd glossed over the fact that I'd clobbered his meth suspect, which I took as a good sign.

At the same time, I'd hinted at the fact that the Chief wasn't really doing any investigating. I was trying to lay the groundwork for later. I'd let the Chief claim credit, as long as he credited us in return. I'd set up a tit for tat that he couldn't refuse, something that would put Creekside Investigations in the spotlight. But first, we had to get to the bottom of what actually happened that night. We needed to learn the truth about Billy's death.

There was an Avery County Sheriff's car in my driveway when I got home. I found Brody and Angelina Will at the dining room table, drinking coffee. Red ran to greet Brody. I hoped that the two women were discussing the case and not me.

"Hey, babe," I said. "Hi, Angelina."

"We've been comparing notes," Brody said.

"About Lees-McRae?" I asked.

"The book club boys confirm Billy's story about having dates with Kate," she began. "Everyone else denies it, but the RA thinks he was at that party. Billy was invited into the cool kid's group, but they didn't want anyone to know about it."

"What's that tell us?" I asked.

"Some kind of cruel joke, we think," Angelina said. "He was at the party to be humiliated. Someone drugged him for sport."

"What about the alleged dates with Kate?" I asked.

"We're not sure about that," Brody said. "Draw him in. Make him comfortable."

"The hot chick is going to go on not one, but two dates with the nerd just to set him up?" I asked. "I'm not buying it."

"Just a thought," Angelina said. "We're open to other ideas if you've got them."

"I don't at the moment," I said. "An hour ago I was wrestling a meth-head in the Valle Crucis wilderness. I've been a bit distracted."

"How did that go?" asked Brody. "Wrestling?"

"Dumb ass charged me," I said. "He was frail and weak and not much of an opponent, but I had to incapacitate him so the cops could pick him up."

Brody gave me a concerned look. I wasn't sure if she was worried about me or chastising me for the physical confrontation.

"He didn't leave me a choice," I said, putting my hands up. "Purely self-defense."

"How bad did you hurt him?"

"He'll have a lump on his head for a while," I said. "Maybe a headache. Three hots and a cot will do him some good, health-wise."

"What did the Sheriff think?"

"He was happy to resolve the matter so quickly," I said. "There are probably more people involved, but they won't want to continue operating in those woods. Plus the perp will likely rat them out."

"What's the world coming to?" Brody asked.

"It used to be moonshine," Angelina said. "Now it's meth. There will always be something cooking in these hollers."

"The underground moonshine trade is dead I take it," I said.

"There are still a few around," she said. "But they make it for themselves and friends. Legal moonshine and liquor stores on every corner did them in."

"Why buy old Charlie's hooch when you can get shine at the ABC?"

"That Gatlinburg stuff may not be authentic shine," she said. "But it's close enough, and it's legal."

"Any meth cooking in your part of the county?" Brody asked.

"It's around," she said. "We see the users, but no busts lately."

"Red can sniff them out if you get a lead," I told her.

I went to take a shower, leaving the women to swap ideas about what happened to Billy Buck. They were still talking when I returned. I fed Red and putzed around, looking for any reason not to sit at the table with them.

"Come on, Breeze," Brody said. "Help us out here."

"You two are the investigators," I said. "I'm just a boat bum."

"Nonsense," Brody said. "You're just as capable as we are. We have got to figure this thing out."

"We're all around the edges of it," Angelina said. "We're missing something though."

"Like why Kate had two dates with the victim," I said. "That's the key. And why we can't twist her arm until she talks."

"If we could get one person to contradict Kate's story, we could put the hammer to her," Angelina said. "So far they all agree. We can't prove that she's lying."

"The book club boys are hearsay," I said.

"Third party information," she said. "It has to be confirmed from at least one other source to be useful."

"What about his parents?" Brody asked.

"Someone that saw them together," she said. "Or knew about it from Kate."

"So where would Kate and Billy go where they wouldn't be seen?" Brody asked. "The boy's father said they went for pizza within walking distance. That could only be the Banner Elk Café."

"Maybe she was seen," Angelina said. "Maybe we're looking at this wrong."

"Not following," I said.

"Some sort of punishment," she said. "Or penance. She was forced to go on a date with Billy because she lost a bet. Or maybe just some silly teenage prank. I don't know."

"Sorority pledge," I said. "It could have been a hazing thing."

"Girls do that shit too?" Brody asked.

"In the guy's version," I said. "The rest of the frat picks out the ugliest girl they can find and forces the pledge to ask her out."

"You could be onto something," Angelina said.

"Sounds like the voice of experience," Brody said.

"I didn't join a fraternity," I said. "I'm not much of a joiner."

"But you saw it in action?" Angelina asked.

"Different frats had different degrees of difficulty," I said. "With some, you have to sleep with the ugly girl."

"God, men are pigs," she said.

"In this case, it looks like women are too," I said. "Present company excluded, of course."

"We need a list of sororities and to find out which one Kate is in," Angelina said. "More people to interview."

"Someone in that club will talk," Brody said. "Someone who doesn't like Kate."

"Or is jealous of her," I added.

"You two are a great team," Angelina said. "It's nice to work with sharp minds."

"Likewise," Brody said. "Don't forget to send some work our way when you get the chance."

"Kate's sorority first," she said. "I'll get a list of names and you can help me track them all down."

"Sounds like ladies work to me," I said. "Me and Red deserve a few days off anyway."

Brody left early the next morning to meet Angelina at Hickermans Country Kitchen for breakfast. I was on my own. I ate a bowl of Captain Crunch because I didn't feel like creating dirty dishes by cooking. Red hung out in front of the fireplace even though there was no fire. He kept eyeing me, waiting for me to take him on another mission or at least play in the yard. I hated to disappoint him, but I had an opportunity to do some thinking with Brody gone. Moonshiners and Meth cookers intrigued me, but I knew little about either. I'd briefly been friends with the son of a famous moonshiner, but his chosen product was marijuana. There was probably a lot of that being grown in these mountains too.

The thing was, I didn't care if some old timer wanted to keep his still running deep in the holler. I didn't care about weed crops growing in the unclaimed wilderness. Meth, on the other hand, drew my ire. It's funny where we all draw our own personal lines. Booze okay, weed okay, meth bad. Still, I stood by that assessment. I could see no good coming from the production of a deadly and sinister drug like meth. Weed didn't hurt anyone. Booze probably hurt plenty, but it was otherwise legal, just like cigarettes. As long as Uncle Sam could tax it, it would remain legal. Why didn't they just do that with weed?

Meanwhile, the girls were down in Banner Elk trying to get sorority girls to talk. Why the hell hadn't I signed up for that gig? Then I recalled that just the previous day, I'd had two pretty women in my house, getting along and playing nice. Naughty thoughts came to mind before I pushed them away. I'd never participated in a threesome, and likely never would. Getting those two working together was an accomplishment in itself. My temptress and my lover were now a team.

Watching them work and spending time with them was reward enough for this old man.

They were much better equipped to deal with teenage girls than I was. They were well aware of the wily ways of young women, and wouldn't be duped by actors, which led me to think about Pat Grant. I knew his type when I was that age. He wasn't the brightest or the best athlete, but he was good enough to weave his way into what he considered the upper echelon. He didn't work that hard either, preferring to ride the coattails of brighter and better students. What he had was confidence. He presented himself as one of the elite. He worked every situation to his advantage. He'd become a banker or politician someday. He couldn't hack the effort that it took to become a lawyer or a doctor.

He'd managed to orchestrate something with Billy and those sorority girls, either for his enjoyment or out of jealousy. He couldn't understand how Billy had infiltrated his group, so he singled him out for punishment. Either that or he was in on it the whole time, played by the girls as a useful idiot. I'd have to deal with Pat Grant eventually. He wouldn't be allowed to escape punishment for his role in Billy's death.

Eight

I pondered having just dealt with two meth users on my most recent jobs. It made me curious as to how serious the problem was in my newly adopted home state. I was surprised by what I found. Meth arrests had been steadily increasing for years. Meth lab busts had increased as well, with the largest concentration coming from the far western counties near where we lived. Thirty to forty labs were being busted each year in Watauga County alone.

There had been a slight downturn in meth activity after North Carolina passed a law restricting the purchase of the main ingredient, pseudoephedrine. The Mexican cartels saw an opportunity and began shipping large quantities of the drug via Atlanta. The new strain was more pure and relatively inexpensive. Meth arrests, deaths, and treatment cases accelerated as a result. Recently, a new method of small batch meth manufacturing popped up in the mountains of western North Carolina. They call it Shake and Bake, and it can be done in small containers such as two-liter bottles. Most production long ago left the cities and suburbs and is now concentrated in the less populated areas. My home turf was a prime area for methamphetamine labs.

I needed to be more aware of this possibility. I spent a lot of time in the woods, often in new parts of the state for me. I wasn't bothered much by the possibility of snakes and bears, but now I needed to keep an eye out for druggies in the wilderness. Pot smokers weren't a violent bunch, but meth users were. Any reasonably thinking person would steer clear of moonshiners for fear of being shot. Suddenly the woods seemed a lot less safe than I'd previously thought.

Now I wanted a smaller handgun that I could conceal during my explorations. My immediate problem was the federally required paperwork. The feds didn't need to know where I lived or that I was purchasing another weapon. I decided to look into opportunities for a private sale. I quickly discovered that my state regulated these purchases heavily. First, you had to go to the county sheriff and obtain a pistol purchase permit. Next, you'd need a concealed carry permit, which required an eight-hour course and a background check. No handgun sales were permitted without meeting these requirements, even among private individuals.

I had good relationships with several sheriffs, but I knew better than to expect them to cut corners for me. They were solid officers of the law. I was certain there had to be a black market for handguns somewhere, but you wouldn't find that on the internet. I'd discuss it with Brody later and see what she thought. Maybe I didn't need another gun that much. It looked to be more trouble than it was worth.

I recall a time when the Second Amendment was all you needed to purchase a gun, but I admit that times have changed. Politics aside, I didn't want to do anything to run afoul of the law in North Carolina. I'd come here for a new start, and with it, I'd formed relationships with surrounding law enforcement. I could have never done either in Florida, hence the move. I was no longer an outlaw. I'd put those days behind me, but that didn't mean I needed my local Sheriff running a background check on me. Thanks to the FBI, the Highway Patrol already knew some of my past. They'd overlooked my previous misdeeds in exchange for my help when needed. They'd grown to appreciate my capabilities. You could say we had an understanding.

I turned my attention away from methamphetamine and back to the death of Billy Buck. We were all sure that the circle of friends around Kate had something to do with it. He was drugged by one of them. We didn't know if they were all in on the scheme or if it was one individual. We didn't know why they did it or what they hoped to gain from it. Brody and Angelina were trying to find out while I diddled around on the internet. I'd gained a new fear of meth-heads and found less respect for the lawmakers of North Carolina, all in twenty minutes or less.

I turned off the computer in disgust. It had been my first extensive use of the damnable machine since we'd bought it. It left me more anxious and less hopeful than I'd been before I started. I couldn't imagine what several hours a day would do to a person. I still felt that machines would be the death of us all someday. I just hoped that it didn't happen until after I was gone.

I was having trouble concentrating on the affairs of the Lees-McRae campus, so I called Red and took him outside to play for a while. I tossed a well-chewed Frisbee for thirty minutes and avoided thinking on the problem. I watched my dog run and jump with glee. He didn't let the worries of the world bother him, no sir. He was an in the moment kind of being. He was happy to be alive and only worried about his next meal. Good for him, I thought. If only we humans worked that way.

There'd been a time when I worried about my next meal, but I also had to worry about the man coming to arrest me or the bad guys coming to shoot me. Moving to the mountains had improved my life in those respects. Working cases in conjunction with the police was a price I was willing to pay for peace of mind. I'd volunteered to do it, as a way to pay back the gods of karma for some of the bad things I'd done in the past. I knew that it would never be enough. I'd keep at this game in one form or another until I died.

Helping Billy's parents come to terms with his death would be a reward in itself. We could almost certainly rule out suicide. At best, it was a tragic accident. At worst it was murder. No conclusion that we could reach would bring him back to life, but knowing for certain that he hadn't killed himself would help Frank and Darla Buck to heal.

The research and the thinking made my brain hurt. I took Red back inside, kicked off my shoes and took a resting position on the couch. Red assumed his normal station in front of the fireplace. Two good old boys took a nice nap until Brody came home. It was a fine way to waste the afternoon.

I opened my eyes when I heard the car pull into the driveway. I felt better when I sat up and came fully awake. My mind was clear. A good nap will do that for you. Brody came in looking encouraged.

"What did you two learn today?" I asked.

"We got the names of most of the girls in Kate's sorority," she said. "Admin still won't give us class schedules or room numbers, but we talked to several of them."

"Get anywhere?"

"One girl knows something," she said. "But wouldn't talk on campus. She didn't want to be seen cooperating with us."

"Did you set up a meeting?"

"Not yet," she said. "She promised to call when she was free."

"If she fails to call, can you take what you have to admin and get her room number?"

"Angelina can," she said. "But the girl was petrified to talk on campus."

"Let's hope she calls, then," I said.

"What did you do today?"

"I learned that there's meth all over these hills," I said. "And that we can't buy a gun without a bunch of red tape, including two permits and another background check."

"Even without concealed carry?"

"First the gun purchase permit," I said. "But you also must have concealed carry to buy a handgun. That comes with an eight-hour class."

"Did you want to buy another gun?"

"I thought about something small for concealment purposes," I said. "But I've changed my mind."

"My forty fits okay in my purse," she said. "Permit or no permit."

"I need to configure my pack so I can get quick and easy access to mine," I said.

"Why the sudden interest in carrying a weapon all over the place?"

"The woods are full of meth labs, apparently," I told her. "The one I found is just down the road from here, and quite close to a public park."

"Do you really think it's a danger?"

"The internet told me so."

"You should only surf the web with adult supervision," she said. "Wait for me next time."

The Banner Elk Chief of Police called that night looking for a progress report. I told him that there was somewhat of a party the night of Billy's death. He was there along with our known suspects. We'd identified someone who may know more, and we were waiting for her call.

"Okay, good," he said. "Keep me apprised."

"Anything else, Chief?"

"There's this thing I thought I could use your help with," he said. "But I don't want to pull you from the campus case."

"Brody and Angelina are working it," I said. "I just handled something for Watauga County the other day. What do you have?"

"A ghillie suit sighting," he said.

"Say again?"

"Some kids from the Grandfather Home were down by Wildcat Creek," he said. "They saw a person go into the woods. First, they thought it was Bigfoot. What they described sounded like a ghillie suit to me."

"Were they approached by this Bigfoot?"

"They ran back to the home and told a counselor," he said. "This person called us. Said he was concerned it was some kind of predator."

"A child predator," I said. "Not the big animal kind of predator."

"Correct."

"That would be a new one on me," I said. "I guess candy doesn't work anymore."

"This isn't a joke, Breeze," he said. "On the other hand, it may have nothing to do with the Grandfather Home."

"A hunter?" I asked. "Militia types?"

"Odd place to hunt or practice for doomsday," he said. "After the school, there's a church camp. Anywhere you go in that piece of woods is close to something."

"The creek comes out of the lake, right?" I said. "Where does it go?"

"It empties into the Elk River," he said. "Not far from Main Street West. Still in town limits."

"Just west of Bodegas a bit?"

"Thick woods south of Main Street," he said. "Nothing down there."

"I've got a general idea," I said. "But why does a man in a ghillie suit let himself get seen by a group of kids? The idea is not to be seen."

"One would think," he said. "Could have been a one-time thing. Guy just trying out his new toy."

"So why send me in there?"

"To show the Grandfather people that we're looking into it," he said. "I can't waste my men's time traipsing around in the woods."

"I don't waste my time for free," I said. "What are you offering me?"

"Go in a couple of times," he said. "Five hundred bucks."

"Okay," I said. "But I'm going to do it right. They won't see me coming or going. Our suspect won't either if he's in there."

"Call for backup if needed," he said. "Don't get into a confrontation."

"You want me to take care of it or not?"

He handed me a pair of handcuffs and a key.

"No guns," he said. "Too many kids in the area. Families at the lake."

"I would assume a ghillie suit wearer would be armed."

"If you see that, call it in," he said. "Track him until we can get to you."

"Understood," I said. "If I don't find him, then at least we know there's no stalker in the woods."

"Assuming you're better than him."

"He let kids see him," I said. "I'm better than him."

I went down into the garage and pulled out my pile of dusty, moldy forest clothes. I hung them on the bushes by the driveway to air out and soak up some mountain scent. I never washed them, preferring they stay dirty. They smelled like the woods. Along with the pants and shirt were a pair of deerskin shoes that an old dope grower had made. He taught me most of what I knew about stealth in the wilderness. He used his skills to tend to his crops without being seen. He'd survived for many years in the wilderness. No one knew he was there. I took the shoes off his dead body and replaced them with my own. I'd left footprints all over his weed patch, and I didn't want to be questioned about his death. When the cops did little to solve the murder, I avenged his death in my own way.

Angelina showed up in the drive and parked behind our car.

"Nice outfit," she said. "Special occasion?"

"Remember when I told you about sneaking through the woods and using Zen and all that?"

"I do," she said. "But what do the dirty clothes have to do with it?"

"They smell like nature," I told her. "Won't give away my scent. They're quiet too, especially the shoes. I can be like a ghost."

"Move like smoke," she said. "I remember. Brody inside?"

"Come on in," I said.

She had a notebook and some paperwork under her arm. She put it all on the table.

"Without the college's help," she began. "It's almost impossible to figure out where these kids might be at any particular time."

"Privacy concerns," Brody said. "We'll have to work around it."

"Back in my day schools had a directory," I said. "Every dorm had at least one copy. Told you what room every student lived in. I once took a road trip to look up a friend from high school. Pulled up on campus, found a directory, and boom; I knew where the girl was."

"Of course it was a girl," Brody said.

"We were just friends," I said. "Teri Smith was her name. She called me Herb."

"Why?" Brody asked. "This ought to be a good story."

"My buddies and I stole a bunch of campaign signs," I said. "A candidate named Herb Gregory offered a reward for our arrest. We stuck all the signs in her parent's yard while the girls were sleeping over."

"I bet they weren't happy about that," Angelina said.

"I got a call from Teri's mom the next morning," I said. "She said she wouldn't collect the reward if we came and removed the signs immediately. We rounded all the signs up and dumped them in the woods way out of town."

"High crimes and misdemeanors," Brody said. "But I don't think Lees-McRae has a directory."

"Just a thought," I said. "Maybe you should hire a teenager to blend in on campus and find out what you need to know."

"And here all this time Brody and I thought we were passing for college kids," Angelina said.

"Maybe grad students," I said.

"Good save," Brody said. "Meanwhile, still no word from our secret witness."

"I'm going to have to talk to a judge," Angelina said. "See if we can't pull these kids in for official questioning."

"Won't they just lawyer up and keep their mouths shut?" I asked.

"Which would give us grounds for suspicion," she said. "If no crime was committed they would talk freely."

"Time to make them understand the seriousness of the situation," Brody said.

"You two have fun with that," I said. "I'll be crawling about the bush near Wildcat Lake."

"You got another job?" Brody asked.

"Two days, five hundred bucks," I said. "For the Banner Elk PD."

"Making headway with the Chief, I see," she said.

"Strange deal," I said. "The mission is tailor-made for me."

"What is it?" Angelina asked.

I told them the story the chief had told me. Looking for a man sneaking around in the woods was my specialty. It was a huge coincidence that this mission would be presented at this time. Was it even real, or did the Chief have some other motive for occupying my time?

"Did you tell him that Angelina and I were still working the campus?" Brody asked.

"Of course," I said. "He acted like it was a nuisance complaint. He'd rather send me out there than waste his time."

"Five hundred bucks is five hundred bucks," Brody said. "And you get to play in the woods."

"As long as it doesn't turn ugly," I said. "But it still beats walking the campus beat."

"You've found enough ways to avoid helping with that," Angelina said. "That's for sure."

"Not my bag," I said. "I have complete confidence in the two of you."

"Creekside Investigations is off to a flying start," she said. "Any more jobs and you'll have to hire help."

"Are you applying for the position?" I asked.

"I'm happy in my current job, thank you," she said. "I don't see this area keeping you in steady work for long anyway."

"Not enough shady business going on?" I asked.

"Crime is low," she said. "The population is low. We've got more cops than we know what to do with, except maybe in Boone."

"We don't need crimes necessarily," I said. "Cheating spouses, disputed wills, business partnerships gone bad. We're not picky."

"I will recommend your services every chance I get," she said. "But I'll keep my day job."

I left them to do their planning while I prepared a pack for the next day's excursion. It had to be light so as not to interfere with my movements. After a while, I gave up on the pack entirely. I decided to carry two bottles of water inside my shirt. I had one snack bar, my phone, and a knife. I could stuff a bandana in my pocket. It could wipe sweat, bandage a wound, or have any number of other uses. That was it. I was traveling light. Satisfied that I was ready for the mission, I returned to the table. The girls were just saying goodbye.

"Be safe tomorrow, Breeze," said Angelina. "See you later."

"Good night," Brody and I said simultaneously.

I waited for Angelina to get in her car and drive away before speaking. I was slightly more comfortable with her presence, but it was still weird. Brody and I were close enough that I felt like I could talk about it.

"Looks like you've got a new friend," I said.

"She's a good person," she responded. "She's smart too. I like her."

"She doesn't make you uncomfortable?"

"Not in the least," she said. "We have a job to do. Does she make you uncomfortable?"

"At first, yes," I admitted. "But I see the two of you working together and getting along. It's not so bad."

"It's not all business," she said. "She thinks you're great. She thinks I'm great. What's not to like?"

"As long as you're happy, I'm happy."

"Stick to that credo, buddy boy," she said. "We'll wrap this up while you're out playing cowboys and Indians."

"I hope you do," I said. "Which one am I?"

"Which what?

"The cowboy or the Indian?"

"You'll always be my cowboy," she said.

"Riding on the range, I got my hat on, boots dusty," I sang. "I got my saddle on my horse. He's called Trigger, of course. I want to be a cowboy, and you can be my cowgirl."

"What the hell is that?"

"Boys Don't Cry," I said. "One hit wonders."

"Can't say that I've heard that one."

"Maybe you prefer Kid Rock," I said. "Cowboy baby, with the top let back and the sunshine shining."

"Please, stop," she said. "You have many talents but singing ain't one of them."

"Just because I can't sing, doesn't mean I won't sing."

"Trust me, cowboy," she said. "You can't carry a tune in a bucket."

"I can't dance either," I said. "But you still love me."

"For many reasons," she said. "Just not your singing and dancing."

I went to bed trying to count the things I was actually good at. I was having a hard time. I could drive a boat, I knew that much, but that skill wasn't required in the mountains. I'd had good luck with the ladies over the years, but now that I'd settled on my one and only, that too seemed like an unneeded attribute. I was a quick thinker, and equally fast on my feet. I could use that. I was more aware of my surroundings than anyone I'd ever met. I was great at being hyper-vigilant. I had a way of getting out of jams, but it was usually trouble of my own making. Things had changed so much. I'd taken a decade's worth of survival skills that had served me well in the underbelly of Florida and moved them to North

Carolina. I was learning, but those old skills didn't always serve me so well here. All I had was my woodland skills. They were new. They seemed natural at times, like I'd been born to them, but I knew better. One slip up, one mistake, and I'd pay for it.

NINE

I drove by the area on Hickory Nut Gap Road. The Grandfather Home was just before Wildcat Lake. There were a dozen or so people at the park. The church camp looked deserted. I circled back past the college's athletic fields and turned left on Tynecastle Highway. I drove through town and turned left again on Main Street. This led me past the downtown campus and out of town. The wilderness area was to my left, but there was no place to leave the car. I turned around and noticed a self-storage lot that had room to park outside the gate.

I sat in the car until no traffic was visible. When I saw my chance, I scrambled across the road and down the hill into the woods. My clothing was like a cloaking device. As long as I moved slowly and carefully, I'd be tough for anyone to spot. I slid deeper into the thick brush before stopping and composing myself. I sat perfectly still and tried to relax. Gradually, I slowed my breathing and heart rate. The sounds of the forest began to come to me, but the traffic noise from the road above dominated them. I crept slowly, deeper into the woods and further from the road.

I made each step with care, not disturbing small twigs or dried leaves that could give me away. I listened carefully for any sound that would betray the presence of another man. I kept my eyes trained for movement. I smelled the air for any hint of soap, shampoo or aftershave. I stayed concealed deep within the vegetation, peering between the leaves and branches at the landscape ahead of me. I wasn't covering ground very fast, but that was not my objective. I had all day to determine if a ghillie-suited man was sharing the woods with me. I realized that he'd be hard to spot as long as he was still, but I was counting on his movement and possibly even his scent.

If he was stationary, he'd set up with a view of the Grandfather Home. That's where he'd last been sighted. I was a long way from there but in no hurry. I couldn't let impatience blow my cover. He could be anywhere if he were there at all. I imagined that most men would feel ridiculous, dressed as I was, sniffing the air and listening to every sound. I felt none of that. I was in my element, becoming one with the woods. It was enlightening to feel the vibrations of nature. I was a tiny speck, but a part of something much larger.

The birds, insects, leaves, and worms were all there to provide clues to my surroundings. The soft dirt, where it was visible, would hold prints for me to examine. Broken twigs would signal an earlier passing by another. Not even the squirrels were alarmed at my presence. I was more animal than man. I let my primitive animal spirit guide me. It took longer than I'd expected, most of the day, to reach a point where I could see the grounds behind Grandfather Home. I moved even slower and with more stealth, sometimes remaining still for ten or fifteen minutes, taking in clues. I did not sense another man in the area.

I made twenty-yards moves along the perimeter of the woods every ten minutes, stopping to smell and listen. Eventually, I was closer to the lake than the Home for Children. I waited there for twenty minutes as it gave me a good view of the entire area. I watched a man fly fish from the dock on the lake. I saw a family test the water with their toes, deciding it was still too cold. Some children came out to play behind the Grandfather School, but remained close to the building. An adult kept a wary eye out for strange men in strange clothes. None of these people had the faintest idea that I was watching them.

I remained where I was until the families left the park and no more children could be seen at the home. Ghillie Man had not come out to play that day, but I didn't give up on my stealth movements. I made a little better time, thinking there was no one to spot me, but I was still careful. When I got back to the road, I hid behind the guardrail until the coast was clear. I crossed undetected and got in the car. The smell of fabric and plastic overwhelmed my nose and pushed away the scents of the woods. It snapped me back to reality and reminded me that I still lived amongst the civilized.

The day hadn't been wasted. I'd learned the lay of the land, and I could move about a little more freely when I returned. Knowing that the man wasn't there, meant that he wasn't a threat to the kids. That didn't mean he wouldn't be there the next time. I made a mental note to bring our pair of compact binoculars back with me. I drove home knowing the job was half done. One more trip and my mission would be complete. I called the Chief to let him know the woods were safe for now.

I was somewhat relieved not to see a police car in the driveway. I liked Angelina, but her presence made me uneasy. Brody was easier to talk to without her being there. I stripped down to my boxers right there in the driveway, hanging my mountain man clothes on the shrubs. I left the deerskin shoes next to the steps and went inside.

"Well hello there, mostly naked man," Brody said in greeting. "I'm fixing dinner, so the funny business is going to have to wait."

"You know the drill," I said. "How was your day?"

"Lees-McRae has a directory," she said.

"So I'm not so stupid after all."

"Only the RAs have it," she said. "And only for their dorms."

"Let me guess," I said. "The sorority girls all live in different dorms."

"For the most part," she said. "Three here, four there."

"How far did you get?"

"One dorm," she said. "These kids don't spend much time in their rooms. We're going to go back at night."

"Campus Gestapo approve of that?"

"I didn't ask," she said. "I've got a cop with me. Provides a little extra leverage."

"What did you learn in that one dorm?"

"Two girls who claimed no knowledge of the night in question," she said. "One who said she'd heard about it, but couldn't offer anything new."

"They're in the sorority, but they don't know about Kate's pledge challenge?"

"It's a big secret, apparently," Brody said. "A regular Greek society omertà."

"Mafia term," I said. "Code of silence."

"Right," she said. "Like the entire campus is protecting these kids."

"That other girl never called?"

"No, but we found out which room she's in," Brody said. "We'll be paying her a visit."

"Something will break," I said. "Sooner or later."

"How did you enjoy playing in the woods today?" she asked.

"It was good, but no one wanted to play," I told her. "There were no creepers around."

"Going back tomorrow?"

"I agreed to two days," I said. "After that, it's on the Chief."

"Get dressed and sit down for dinner," she said. "Angelina is picking me up at seven."

"A night home alone," I said. "I might have to break out the whiskey and howl at the moon."

"Let Red do the howling," she said. "I've heard your singing."

"I just might do that," I said. "Build us a fire out back and watch the stars."

"Save me a spot," she said. "Should be home by ten or eleven."

"I will if I can stay awake that long," I said.

"Go easy on the whiskey then," she said.

Angelina arrived promptly at seven. As soon as the two women left, I went out to the woodpile and carried some logs to our fire pit behind the house. Red thought I wanted to play fetch. He kept grabbing at the logs and waiting for me to throw one. The logs were a bit large to be used as play toys, so I found a stick and threw it as far as I could. I rounded up some kindling, but before I could get a fire going, I had to throw the stick for twenty minutes. Finally, my dog gave me a break, and soon I had a blaze roaring. He sat down with me and chewed on that stick contentedly.

The sun was gone, and the sky grew dark. It was a rare cloudless night, so millions of stars were visible. The winter had been gray and gloomy. The rain had dampened nearly every day until recently. It was finally full spring in the mountains, much later than down in the valleys. I stared at the flames and poked the wood with my own stick. Red fell asleep at my feet.

Contemplating the night sky can make a man feel small. I used to think like that while underway far out in the Gulf of Mexico. The sea and the endless sky dwarf our meager existence. I am but a speck of dust in the infinite universe, yet I am alive. I have hopes and dreams that give me meaning. I have a woman I love to share it with. Life wasn't so bad. I'd been down, but I'd never given up. Here in our mountain hideaway, I could relax and appreciate how far I'd come.

After philosophizing about the meaning of life for a while, I turned my thoughts to the matters at hand. I'd been left out of the Billy Buck investigation. The girls were doing their best, but I thought maybe I should intervene somehow, shake things up a bit. I was losing patience with the stubborn refusal of the students to tell the truth. Maybe I could make a dent in their self-important attitudes with a little crude reality. The cops wouldn't like it, but something needed to be done. I was a man of action, and all this sitting around doing nothing was wearing thin.

Meanwhile, there may or may not have been a strange man stalking the woods near the Grandfather Home in severe camouflage. That was an odd one. I hadn't given much weight to it being a real threat. Instead, I'd leaned towards some guy trying out his new stuff, not thinking about his proximity to innocent children. A quick talk with a stern warning would be all it took to send him packing, if he showed up again. If that was indeed the case, it was probably a one-time occurrence, and there was no need to worry. If I came up empty the next day, I'd forget about the whole thing.

Red was chasing rabbits in his dreams, so I was careful not to disturb him when I got up to get more wood. We'd used most of our supply over the winter, and it was time to start preparing for the winter to come. At first, splitting and stacking wood felt good. It truly helped me to transition to mountain life. Eventually, it became work, especially after it got cold. I vowed to split and stack enough for an entire winter while it was still warm. I also wanted to get the chimney swept before we needed to burn wood again.

I'd barely touched the whiskey, but I was running out of deep thoughts to ruminate on, so I increased my efforts. Soon I had a warm glow inside to match what the fire provided on the outside. My thoughts got a little fuzzy, so I gave up thinking. I was asleep in the lawn chair when Angelina dropped Brody off.

"Wake up, both of you," Brody said. "You can sleep in the house."

"Sorry, babe," I said. "Long day I guess."

She picked up the half-empty bottle of whiskey from the ground beside my chair.

"Yeah," she said. "That was probably it."

I shook Red awake and followed her inside. Our big comfy bed was calling my name.

"Go ahead," she said. "I'll fill you in tomorrow."

"You're an angel," I said. "Good night."

The dreams came quickly. I had barely put my head down when I saw Pat Grant sending Billy over the edge of the spillway. Billy could barely walk, drunk with a date rape drug. Grant held him up as he instructed him to walk across the narrow ledge atop the spillway. He laughed like a demon when Billy went over the side and onto the rocks below. I saw a gaggle of teenage girls on the hill behind him, laughing like hyenas.

Before I could make sense of what I'd witnessed in that dream, I saw the Ghillie Man snatch a child from the playground at the Grandfather Home. The little girl kicked and screamed, but no one heard her except me. Her abductor was invisible to everyone else. I saw him until he made the wood line, then he was gone. I ran after him and thrashed through the brush looking, but he was gone, along with the little girl. Brody shook me awake.

"Are you okay?"

"Just dreams," I said. "But I'm getting up for a bit. Go back to sleep."

I relocated to the couch so I wouldn't keep her up. Red came and lay on the floor below me, sensing something was up. I rubbed his ears for a long time, until I was sleepy enough to lie down again. My dog remained with me, keeping guard throughout the rest of the night. I'd forgotten the dreams when I woke up, but Brody reminded me over breakfast. I'd had serious problems with nightmares in the past, and she was worried that it would happen again.

"I'll be fine once we dispense with these cases," I told her. "I promise."

"What about when we get new cases?"

"I'll deal with it as it comes," I said. "They're just dreams."

"No, it's more than that," she suggested. "Somehow you invest too much of yourself in whatever we're dealing with at the time."

"Some call that dedication," I offered.

"Some call it an obsession," she countered.

"What does Doctor Brody suggest?"

"Take a break," she said. "Let's go do something fun. Go out to eat; maybe see some live music."

"Today I give the Chief his second day on the other side of town," I said. "And we need to make some real progress on that campus. Finish up the job we promised to do. Then we can have our fun."

"All work and no play makes for a very dull Breeze."

"It will be over soon," I said. "Then we'll turn down any jobs that come our way until we've had sufficient play time."

"Our night visit to campus was a bust," she said. "The girl we hoped to talk to wasn't in her room. The others all had the same attitude. We didn't get anything new."

"Did Angelina talk to a judge yet?" I asked. "Why aren't we putting the screws to these kids?"

"The Avery County judiciary is not inclined to issues subpoenas without physical evidence or witness testimony," she said. "We've got to get someone to talk."

"The physical evidence is a dead kid with Rohypnol in his system," I said. "Seems pretty clear to me."

"No physical evidence or witness corroboration that connects any of our suspects," she said.

"I see bright lights and rubber hoses," I said. "Waterboarding, electrical shock."

"You know we can't do that," she said.

"Maybe a few well-placed knuckle sandwiches."

"That's not justice, and you know it," she said.

"I'm not so sure anymore," I said. "Let me do my thing today, and we'll talk about this later."

"Be careful out there," she said. "You never know."

I left the cabin full of fury, wanting to slap around some college kids until they talked, but I had other obligations. I drove down to Banner Elk, through the campus, and on to the outskirts of town. I parked at the self-storage place again and waited for a good opportunity to cross the road. Once I got over the guardrail, and down into the woods, I felt better. I calmed myself and concentrated on the day's job. I put those cocky college kids out of my mind and focused on the woods in front of me. This was my refuge. Even though I had a job to do, I was at home in this environment. I made it my single reason for being that day. All outside thoughts were dismissed. I had a Ghillie Man to find.

Ten

It took longer than usual to control all of my faculties. I sat hidden in the weeds, slowing my breathing for thirty minutes. When I was ready, when the forest finally spoke to me, I started making slow progress towards the target area. I was able to ignore the road noise until it faded into oblivion behind me. I crept and crawled from tree to rock. I scanned my field of vision constantly, aware of everything. I'd brought our binoculars, and used them to good measure at each stopping point. My sense of smell was on alert for anything not part of the woods.

This time I circled to the side of the lake closer to the church camp. I hugged the edge of the woods as I moved towards Grandfather Home. I stopped every twenty yards to scan my field of view for movement. There were no children outside playing. A few people stood near the edge of the lake. I did not see a camouflaged man hiding in the weeds, but I crept on. Before I reached the spot I was shooting for; I heard someone coming. They walked carelessly, snapping twigs and breathing hard. I wedged myself deep into the bushes and looked through my binoculars.

A man stopped and knelt, removing his backpack. I watched as he removed the preposterous ghillie suit from the pack. He had a hard time getting into the thing, and he looked like Sigmund the Sea Monster when he was done. Only when he got on all fours and started a slow crawl did I appreciate the effectiveness of it. If he remained still, he'd be almost impossible to spot. He hadn't, to this point, snuck through the woods and given himself away. Of course, he had no reason to believe that he shared the woods with anyone else. I tracked him to the edge of the brush, where he stopped, facing the back of the children's home.

I let him get comfortable before leaving my hiding place. I slid through the brush on furry feet, making soft steps that made no sound. I was slow and silent, slithering among the trees like a snake. Pop Sutton would have been proud of me. I was smoke, floating on the breeze. The stalking man never heard me coming. He lay there in the tall grass watching the playground. I could have reached out and touched him before he knew I was there. Instead, I jumped him. I had a cuff around one wrist before he could put up resistance. He tried to roll away, but I had the other cuff in my hand. I used it to twist his arm behind his back, shoving his face into the dirt at the same time. He tried to push himself up with the other hand, allowing me to grab it and complete the cuffing. He was finished then. In the heavy suit, he couldn't even get up off the ground.

"Sit tight pal," I said. "Your ride will be here soon."

"What are you doing?" he asked. "Who the hell are you?"

"Just a concerned citizen," I told him. "Protecting and serving and shit."

"How'd you sneak up on me like that?" he asked. "Where did you come from?"

"Unlike you, I have skills of the stealth kind."

"I was just playing around here," he said. "Seeing how the suit works."

"It didn't stop me from finding you," I said. "I hope you kept the receipt."

I let him lay there face down while I called the Chief. He had an officer at the abandoned hospital, which wasn't far away.

"Directly behind the Grandfather Home," I said. "At the edge of the woods."

I knelt behind the fallen, handcuffed man, careful to avoid any kicks he might launch at me. I got a good grip on the center of the cuffs and pulled.

"On your feet, asshole," I said.

He wasn't a big man, and he hadn't put up much of a fight. When I think of suits like the one he wore, I thought of Navy Seals and snipers and such. This guy was nothing of the sort. He didn't attempt to escape at all. I saw the cop come around the building so I started marching my captive into the open field so that we could be easily seen. The officer waved in acknowledgement before reaching for his weapon.

We met halfway, and I gave my guy a little shove towards the officer.

"These are the Chief's handcuffs back," I said. "Only used once."

"Good work, Breeze," he said. "Can you come down to the station and talk to the Chief about what you saw him doing?"

"My car is over on West Main at the storage facility," I said. "Come with me then. I'll give you a ride back after we book this guy."

The prisoner looked ridiculous trying to get into the backseat of the patrol car in his get-up. The officer was kind enough to pull the hood down to give him some breathing room. It's not every day a cop gets to book Sigmund the Sea Monster. It took both of us to help him out once we arrived at the police station. The Chief looked on with an amused look as we brought him inside.

"Considering that this man is likely a disgusting pervert," he said. "I shouldn't laugh. But damn he looks silly. Good work, Breeze."

"What happens to him now?" I asked.

"We'll listen to his story," the Chief said. "Then we'll scour the laws to figure out what to charge him with."

"Is stalking a crime?"

"Yes it is," he said. "But it's a misdemeanor that might get him probation. Aggravated stalking is a felony, but that means it violates a protective order, which isn't the case here."

"We know he did it at least twice," I said. "If that makes a difference."

"If he didn't cause any harm or emotional distress he'll get a slap on the wrist," he said. "He'll be barred from being near the Grandfather Home. He'll have a probationary period. Get his name in the paper."

"So this was all for nothing?"

"Of course not," he said. "We'll figure out who he is, check him for warrants and priors. If he's a repeat offender, maybe we can lock him up. You protected those kids today, Breeze. It wasn't for nothing."

"Thanks," I said. "That makes me feel a little better."

"What's the latest on campus?" he asked.

"The girls are running into nothing but resistance," I said. "Lips are sealed tight."

"Is campus security giving them any trouble?"

"Not that I'm aware," I said. "It's the kids themselves. They're all stonewalling, waiting for it to go away."

"Avery County isn't going to let their detective stay on the case forever," he said. "She's going to need to get somewhere soon."

"No one wants to taint the reputation of the college," I said. "Judges are wary; the school administration won't cooperate. Kids who weren't involved won't talk. It's a closed society protecting itself."

"You've been busy with other things," he said. "Maybe it's time for you to take a more active role."

"I've been thinking the same thing," I said. "Give us a little longer."

"I'm not going anywhere," he said. "Just letting you know you need to make something happen soon."

The arresting officer came back out and offered me the ride to my car. He didn't have much to say during the drive. I got the impression that he knew something about our offender that he didn't care to share. I was too tired to worry about it. I'd done my job, and I just wanted to go home. He pulled into the parking lot and let me out.

"Nice work today," he said. "Saved us all a lot of grief."

"Anytime," I said. "Take it easy."

I drove home feeling a bit let down. The Ghillie Man had not been a worthy adversary. Unless he had prior arrests for the same type of thing he'd walk out a free man. It all seemed like a waste of time, other than protecting the children. I suppose that should be good enough, but with Billy's Bucks death still unresolved, I had little sense of accomplishment. I was completely out of patience with the situation on campus. I needed a good night's sleep, and then I would take matters into my own hands.

Brody reported some slight progress when I got home. A girl had whispered a message in passing near the campus bar.

"Pat Grant did it," she said.

"Drugged Billy or killed him?" Brody asked, but the girl kept walking and didn't respond.

"I always thought he was at the center of it," I said. "I'm going to go have another talk with him."

"What makes you think he'll change his story now?" she asked. "He's got the whole school covering for him."

"I'll be using a different approach this time," I said. "Leave it to me."

"I barely got a look at this new girl," she said. "She had already passed me when she whispered."

"Why didn't you chase her down?"

"She already risked being a pariah," she said. "But there may be more like her."

"The Chief warned me time is running out," I said. "Either he is being impatient, or we're wearing out our welcome at Lees-McRae."

"As if we were ever welcomed in the first place," she said. "All the girls are like little Stepford Wives."

"So who's the power behind the clique?" I asked. "Does Pat Grant control the girls or are the girls pulling his strings?"

"I'd say Kate is the ringleader," she said. "But who knows what a boy would be capable of if he was trying to get close to her."

"So Kate's a manipulative cunt toying with Billy," I began. "Grant wants to impress her, so he dopes Billy's drink to amplify the fun. It all goes wrong somehow, but they band together to keep it covered up."

"Why cover for Grant if he's an outlier?" she asked.

"Because he knows the game," I said. "The girls are just as responsible as he is."

"How do we get to them?"

"I'll let you know as soon as I figure it out," I said.

That wasn't really the truth. I had made up my mind as to a plan of action. I was going to have a little man to man with Mr. Pat Grant. Brody wouldn't be there to see it. Sometimes it took a man to do a man's job. I turned in early and got a good night's sleep. My mind was clear, which kept the dreams at bay.

Brody's look questioned me over breakfast, but I didn't bite. The less she knew, the better. Angelina was picking her up, leaving me our car. I waited for them to leave before preparing to visit the campus myself. I limbered up some, readying myself for a scuffle. I visualized how it might go. Grant had a few inches on me and a few pounds. He was much younger, but too young to know what a real fight meant. I wasn't your average middle-aged man when it came to violence. My biggest worry would be not hurting him too badly. He was about to suffer shock and awe, which I hoped would make him talk.

I drove slowly on the way to town, enjoying the scenery and smelling the spring blooms that had sprouted everywhere along my route. I felt good because I had a purpose that day. I was reverting to something that I understood quite well. I was taking swift, decisive action instead of sitting back and letting things happen around me. The women had their chance; now it was my turn. It wasn't a sophisticated plan, but it was what I knew.

I stood in front of his door and knocked.
"Who is it?"
I knocked again, with more urgency. I was ready when the door cracked open. I used it as a battering ram, smashing it into the kid with maximum force. I was through the doorway and on top of him before he realized what was

going on. I kicked the door shut and planted a fist square on his nose. It was a good solid blow that caused things to crack and blood to flow. I yanked him up by his collar and threw him into his desk. His computer crashed to the floor along with assorted college kid paraphernalia. He managed to get to one knee before I kicked him in the kidney.

He put a hand up in surrender.

"What the fuck are you doing, man?" he asked.

"Wiping that smirk off your punk face," I said. "I've got questions that need answers."

"I've answered everyone's questions," he said.

I responded with a quick kick to his other kidney. He balled up in the floor with his arms protecting his head.

"The truth," I said. "How did Billy Buck die?"

"He got stupid drunk and fell off the spillway," he said. "That's all I know."

"Were you the one that drugged him?"

"I don't know anything about that," he said.

His kidneys had suffered enough damage. My right hand hurt a little from smacking him in the face, so I used my left hand to club one ear. He wailed in pain but refused to change his story. Now both of my hands hurt. He was a hard-headed son of a bitch. Someone banged on his door.

"You all right in there, Pat?"

"This crazy fucker attacked me," Grant yelled. "I need help."

Rampmeyer the RA entered the room and gasped at what he saw. He turned and ran out, but I saw him going for his phone. The cops or campus security would show up soon, leaving me no time for an extended torture session. I had felt certain that he would talk after being knocked around a little, but he fooled me. There was no point in waiting around to be arrested for assault, so I bolted.

"I can get to you anytime I want," I told him on my way out. "But the truth will set you free."

"Fuck you, asshole," he responded.

As soon as I got to the car, I regretted what I'd done. Everyone would be pissed at me, most especially Brody. There was a good chance we'd be kicked off campus permanently, ruining our chances to finally solve the mystery. That Grant bastard hadn't caved like I expected him to. Was I wrong about him?

I confessed to Brody as soon as I got home. Before she could scold me too much, the Chief pulled into our driveway.

"You can let him in," she said. "I'll go pack your toothbrush."

The Chief was calm when he came into our cabin. He took his hat off and gave me an exasperated look.

"What the fuck, Breeze?"

"I know," I said. "It was a stupid thing to do."

"Did the kid tell you anything?"

"Stuck by his story," I said. "Stupid and fruitless."

"We'll see if he wants to file a complaint," he said. "In the meantime, you are forbidden from stepping foot on that campus."

"What about Brody?"

"Did she beat up a freshman student?" he asked.

"She wasn't there," I said. "Didn't know anything about it."

"She's to be accompanied by Deputy Will at all times," he said. "I still want this thing solved."

"You're not arresting me?"

"Not yet," he said. "Depends on how much the kid whines and if he lawyers up. If he presses charges, then I'll be back to see you."

"I appreciate the leniency," I told him. "Even if it is only temporary."

"I'd smack some sense into him too if I thought I could get away with it."

"I thought he'd talk," I said.

"Maybe he's telling the truth."

Brody stared me down with her hands on her hips. I knew what she was going to say.

"How can someone so smart do something so stupid?" she asked.

"I've got no defense," I said. "You're right to be angry."

"We're not in some back alley in Fort Myers Beach," she said. "We're not dealing with bums in the mangroves. We're trying to build a reputation as helpful to law enforcement. Beating up teenagers is not part of the plan."

"I just knew that he'd talk if I pushed him hard enough," I said. "I was wrong."

"You'll be lucky not to get arrested," she said. "Then we can kiss our business goodbye."

"He must be telling the truth," I said. "There's no other explanation."

"Pat Grant wasn't a part of Billy's death?"

"The girls must have done it without his help," I said. "They drugged him. They somehow led him to his death. Grant didn't do it."

"How could he not know about it?"

"I don't know; he left maybe," I said. "Billy started acting weird, so he bugged out. Whatever happened next was the girl's fault, and they are the only ones who know."

"You want to go down there and beat up a few of them?"

"Don't be ridiculous," I said. "Maybe I keyed in on Grant because he was the man of the group. Men should be leaders. Then I used man logic to try to get him to talk."

"Neanderthal man logic maybe," she said.

"I got impatient with female intuition not solving the case," I said. "No offense intended."

"So you decided to bust some heads," she said. "How evolved of you."

"I already admitted I was wrong," I said. "Bear with me here. The girls drugged him, not Pat Grant."

"To what end?" she asked. "More humiliation?"

"My question is did they really want to kill him?" I said. "Or did things simply get out of hand."

"Why would they want him dead?"

"Kate had some sort of relationship with him as part of a prank, or hazing," I said. "How far did she have to take it? She passed her little test, but there was one thing left hanging. Billy could tell his friends. Word could get out. Suddenly, Billy had to go."

"She slept with him then killed him so that he couldn't tell?" she asked. "Sounds like a bad movie plot."

"Truth is stranger than fiction," I said.

"Just to play along," she began. "There would have to be a limited number of sorority girls that knew about it. The initiators would be upperclassmen. The leaders of the sorority."

"They may have tasked her with boinking the dork," I said. "But not necessarily killing him. She could have taken that route on her own."

"Only her closest confidantes would know."

"But would they?" I asked. "Billy is left alone with Kate after being drugged. Everybody is gone. She does the deed, verifying it somehow, then offs him."

"Now I feel like smashing her pretty little face," Brody said.

"Just a theory," I said. "It's up to you and Angelina to find out."

"Thanks to your foolishness."

"God has a special providence for fools, drunkards, and the United States of America, I said.

"That doesn't sound biblical."

"Otto Van Bismarck," I said.

"How do we prove Kate acted alone?" she asked. "With no witnesses, it seems impossible."

"Make up a witness," I suggested. "Tell her you know what happened."

"I'll run that by Angelina," she said. "But I think you may be on to something. Who the hell is Otto Van Bismarck?"

"The Iron Chancellor of Germany in the late 1800s," I said. "Widely considered a political genius."

"How do you know these things?"

"I wasn't always a boat bum," I said.

"My man Breeze," she said. "Educated and well-read, but still a caveman at heart."

"Look, I apologize again for today," I said. "But I thought that I could intimidate the truth out of that kid. I was wrong, but it's led us in a different direction. Maybe we can get to the bottom of this yet."

"Officially, I'm still mad at you," she said. "But off the record, I can't stay mad for long."

"If the Chief comes back to take me in, you're welcome to revisit that sentiment."

"Damn straight I am," she said.

Eleven

Pat Grant made a lot of noise about being afraid for his life, but he didn't press charges. He told his family and friends that he intended to transfer to Appalachian State once the semester ended. The Chief forced me to swear on all things holy that I wouldn't harass the kid, or be seen anywhere near him. I was still forbidden from campus. Red and I got restless sitting around doing nothing. Brody and Angelina had so far failed to come up with a plan to entrap Kate. I kept my mouth shut about the matter, having already screwed things up once.

I abandoned the fly rod I'd once given Pop Sutton. I drove all the way to Bristol to visit the Bass Pro Shops, where I purchased a fine St. Croix ultralight spinning rod. I paired it with a sweet little Shimano reel and loaded up on lures and goodies to harass trout with. I'd seen enough of the lakes and rivers in the area to begin my quest to catch some decent fish on light spinning tackle. I only had to learn the differing rules that governed each body of water. I almost needed a lawyer at my side to know what lures I could use, when I could fish, and if I could keep any fish or not.

To get the feel of things, I chose Wildcat Lake as my first destination. I'd been all around the edges of it stalking the stalker in a ghillie suit. I knew I could get away from the park area and still have access to cast for trout. I caught a few small ones that didn't quite satisfy my thirst. I moved on to Beech Mountain over the next several days, trying the waters of Buckeye and Coffey lakes. It was nice to get out and not be working for someone. The fishing was mediocre, but it took my mind off things. That is until Pat Grant changed his mind. His parents found out about my assault and convinced him to have me arrested.

I can only imagine the conversations that went on as to who would come pick me up. The crime took place in Banner Elk, which is in Avery County. They could have sent Angelina to put me in cuffs, or the Chief could have done it himself. I didn't live within the boundaries of either Avery County or Banner Elk, so they called on my old friend Rominger, with the Highway Patrol. He was friendly about it, aside from the lecture I received on the way to the courthouse in Newland. He didn't make me wear cuffs for the ride, and I sat in the front seat with him. When we pulled into the parking lot, he apologized before making me wear the cuffs inside to be booked.

I had my mug shot and fingerprints taken, which I didn't like too much, but there was nothing I could do about it. I was about to pop up on some government employees radar. The FBI would know of my arrest. I didn't think I had any outstanding warrants, but I sweated it for a while. The charge was simple assault, due to the victim not seeking medical treatment. As a first offender, I was eligible for probation. I pled guilty and waived my right to counsel, hoping for leniency. I just wanted to get it over with, and not suffer an actual trial. The judge had the ability to hand down my sentence on the spot, which he did.

"Would you care to explain why you attacked a college student unprovoked?" he asked.

"I had reason to believe he took part in a crime that led to the death of another student," I said.

"In what capacity were you acting when you came upon this information?"

"Private Investigator, your honor," I said.

"Was this an attempt to beat a confession out of the victim?"

"I guess you could say that," I admitted. "He refused to cooperate with our questioning."

"Our questioning?"

"There are two of us that make up Creekside Investigations," I said. "And we were working alongside an Avery County Deputy."

"Deputy Will, I understand."

"That's correct, your honor," I said.

"She was just here to speak on your behalf," she said. "She took partial blame for your mistaken opinion about the victim. She initially agreed that he was withholding evidence."

"We're leaning the other way now," I said. "I was wrong, and it won't happen again."

"Without the word of an officer of the law, I'd be inclined to give you thirty days," he said. "Two weeks minimum, but on her voucher, I sentence you to one day in jail, a fine of five hundred dollars, and one-year probation."

I suppose that one day in jail was supposed to teach me a lesson. It was a bit of an inconvenience, but I'd live. The additional ping to my criminal record was what I didn't like, but I only had myself to blame. I was able to ask Rominger to let Brody know that I wouldn't be home for dinner.

"No problem, brother," he said. "The judge will see you again around nine in the morning. I'll let her know to pick you up."

"Thanks, man," I said. "Sorry to put you through this."

"You should have learned how to stay out of trouble by now," he said.

"Slow learner, I guess."

I was put in a holding room to await transport to the Avery County Jail. They took my phone, my belt, and my shoelaces. They offered me a phone call, but I didn't know Brody's number. They wouldn't let me look at my phone to retrieve it. At least I knew that Rominger would fill her in. I sat there for over an hour, when Deputy Angelina Will arrived.

"Are you the paddy wagon or just here to visit?" I asked.

"Both," she answered. "You ready to take a ride?"

"It would be quicker to walk," I said. "The jail is just down the street."

"I had a slight detour in mind," she said.

"I'm not sure how to respond to that," I said.

Was she making another move to get me in the sack? I thought we'd gotten past that, but this would be a perfect opportunity. I was literally a captive audience. I'd have a hard time resisting her advances while in handcuffs. Part of me thought maybe that might be a good time. The little devil on my left shoulder was all in. *Let her have her way with you.* The little angel on my right shoulder had a different opinion. *Brody, dumbass. You won't cheat on Brody, handcuffed or not.*

As it turned out, my thinking was completely off track. Angelina took me for a little drive to discuss the Lees-McRae affair, not the Angelina and Breeze affair. I felt like an idiot when I realized what she wanted. It wasn't my body.

"Talked to Brody about your new take on Pat Grant," she said. "We both agree that there's a good chance that Kate is the sole perpetrator."

"But you haven't decided how to get an admission out of her."

"We're not going to beat it out of her," she said. "Dumbass."

"I deserved that," I said.

"She said something about inventing a witness."

"Old FBI tactic," I said. "You tell Kate that someone saw her at the spillway with Billy."

"But what if she wasn't there when he fell?"

"Then she'll tell you where she was instead," I said. "She'll slip up, trying to protect herself."

"If she's guilty."

"If she's not then we suck as investigators," I said. "Who else could it be?"

"It has to be her," she said. "But you thought that about Pat Grant."

"So far you've gotten nowhere trying to get her friends to rat her out," I said. "Maybe they don't know what happened."

"Your theory is that she was left alone with Billy," she said. "So there were no witnesses."

"Still only a theory," I said. "You'll have to get Kate to break if you want to prove it."

"By inventing a witness," she said.

"It would help if Kate were in a holding cell for interrogation," I said. "Make her stew in her juices for a couple of hours. Lay the witness story on her. Tell her what happens to pretty girls in prison."

"You've been watching too many detective shows," she said. "This is the real world. It's rural North Carolina for crying out loud."

"I rarely watch television," I said. "And I thought you wanted to be like those TV detectives. Here's your shot."

"I knew you'd bring that up," she said. "You're too smart for your own good sometimes."

"So I've been told," I said. "Then I go and do something so horribly dumb they all forget how smart I'm supposed to be."

"At least you're self-aware," she said. "I'll give you that much."

"I think I do it just so I don't get too big for my britches," I said. "Subconsciously maybe."

"Interesting psychological take," she said. "You could publish a paper on it."

"That's a discussion for another day," I said. "I'm supposed to be in a jail cell right now. You seem to be looking to me for advice. This is your case now. Go rattle Kate's psyche. Set her up to fail. Play the hardboiled detective role like you've always wanted. Marshal all the available resources and all of your knowledge and experience. This is the case that gets Angelina Will on the map."

"Thanks for the lecture," she said. "But you're right. That's damn good advice. I can do this."

"Damn right you can," I said. "Can you also check on Brody tonight? I'll be okay. Just make sure she's okay."

"Will do," she said. "Sorry but I've got to tuck you in for the night."

"Thanks for the ride."

Angelina put the cuffs back on me and led me into the jail. She knew the guards and staff, and asked them to go easy on me. She told them she'd be back in the morning to take me to the courthouse. My one-day prison sentence would last from six at night until nine the next morning. I didn't even have a toothbrush, and I wasn't given one. I got placed in the drunk tank with metal bunks along one wall and an open toilet. I had two roomies, both sleeping it off on their chosen bed. I hadn't eaten, and no one offered me a meal. I must have missed chow time while riding around with Angelina.

It turned out to be a very long night. Not being at home with Brody and Red was a shock to my system. There was no beer or whiskey to prepare me for bedtime. I had no reading material or television. Boredom overtook me within an hour. I sat on a bunk with my back to the wall feeling sorry for myself. I'd been through worse, but the indignity of the situation was tough to take.

One of the other prisoners got up and walked around the cell. He stopped in front of me and asked me what I was in for.

"Assault," I said, trying to look and sound tougher than I was.

"How long?"

"I'm supposed to see the judge tomorrow morning," I said.

"Me too," he said. "Good luck."

"For you too," I said. "Drunk driving?"

"I've been drunker," he said. "But I didn't get caught."

"If it's your first time then maybe they'll go easy on you," I said.

"If I lose my license, I'm fucked," he said. "A man's got to get to work. What do you do?"

"Private investigator," I said. "And part-time tracker."

"Tracker?" he asked.

"I've got a fantastic hound dog," I said. "But I can find a man on my own when necessary."

"I thought that was a forgotten art," he said. "Folks don't even run coons anymore."

"The dog came to me as a stray," I said. "He was already trained. I'd handled a few tracking jobs, so it just seemed natural to add him to the team."

"The team?"

"My gal Brody was FBI," I told him. "Creekside Investigations."

"So if you're a private eye, with FBI connections, what are doing in the Avery County jail with us drunks?"

"Good question," I said. "Stupid acts have consequences."

"I drive home from the bar under the influence damn near every night," he said. "This one time I get pulled over. You do one dumb thing and we get to spend the night together. Kind of levels the playing field don't it?"

"My name's Breeze," I said. "It's not my first night behind bars."

"Ford," he said. "My friends call me Whitey."

"Whitey Ford?"

"Played a little ball in high school," he said. "Big fish in a small pond. I had dreams of playing pro, but I wasn't near good enough."

"No kidding," I said. "Same here. I got signed and sent to the rookie league in Texas. Didn't last long there. Ended up playing Mexican ball for a few years."

"Mexican ball?" he asked. "How was that?"

"The games were fun," I said. "The money was bad. My teammates liked me well enough, but the rest of them hated the gringo. I picked up a little Spanish. Dated a cute Mexican girl. Overall it was a good experience."

"You got farther than I ever did," he said. "Couldn't afford college. Started working at the sawmill right out of high school."

Talking to my new friend Whitey Ford helped to pass the time. I wanted to give him my card, but they were in my wallet. We talked about the glory days gone by until I finally got sleepy. I ignored the crusty blanket and managed to finally drift off. The other guest in our little hotel never stirred. I knew that he was alive when I woke to the sounds and smells of him taking a shit on the open toilet. I refused to look. I didn't want that image stuck in my head for the rest of my life.

After I got up, I started to fret over having to use that toilet myself. Normally, a cup of coffee would get things moving in the morning. I'd retire to my private bath and take care of business behind a closed door. That wouldn't be possible here. When coffee was offered, I refused. I had two hours before seeing the judge. It was almost another hour drive to get home. Could I hold out that long? The morning pooper was named Rico. He'd been through this routine a dozen times he told me. He also said that we'd all be brought into court at the same time. I might be first, or I might be last. There would be other cases on the docket besides the three of us. This lessened the chances that I'd be able to make it home to take a dump. I had to laugh at myself. There I was sitting in a jail cell, and all I was worried about was being able to poop in private.

I was relieved to see Angelina appear at the cell door. I was starting to experience some discomfort. She took me alone out of there, leaving my roommates behind.

"A van will be here shortly," she told them. "Sit tight."

Rico grumbled. Whitey gave me a thumbs up.

"The judge will see you first," Angelina said. "Brody is already at the courthouse."

"Thanks for this," I said. "Anyway, can we stop at a restroom first?"

"Sorry, no can do," she said. "You're getting a private session before the doors open. We can't be late."

I was given my belongings and escorted into the judge's chamber. Brody and Angelina came in with me. I was instructed to sit.

"Good people have contacted me on your behalf, Mr. Breeze," the judge said. "I understand that you have assisted law enforcement on several occasions, even being credited with saving lives. That's why we are expediting your release this morning."

"Thank you, your honor."

"Now you understand that these people have faith in you," he said. "And the burden you now bear in not betraying that trust?"

"I do."

"You've already spent your night in jail," he said. "And I've already given you one year's probation in open court. The best I can do is to make that probation unsupervised. You won't have to report, and it will automatically expire after the year is up, provided you don't have another lapse in judgment. Do you understand?"

"I understand."

"You're a free man, Mr. Breeze," he said. "Don't fuck it up."

"Thank you, sir," I said. "I won't."

On our way out we passed the other two prisoners. I slipped Whitey our business card. Brody and Angelina hustled me out of the courthouse.

"You okay?" Brody asked.

"I'm good, but get me home fast," I said. "I'm about to poop my pants."

Both women laughed at me, but I was dead serious.

"Hurry up," I said. "Let's roll."

We said our goodbyes to Angelina and headed home. I almost made it. The turbulence became too much to stand. I made Brody pull into the Food Lion parking lot. She waited in the car while I ran inside to the restroom. It wasn't my own private bathroom, but at least there was a door on the stall. Relief came fast and furious. I was going to be okay. I washed my hands and picked up a half-dozen Krispy Kremes on the way out.

"Take me home, darling," I said. "I need a cup of coffee and a hot shower."

"I hope you've learned your lesson," she said.

"One night of that was enough," I told her. "The toilet was in the middle of the room for crying out loud. What kind of barbarian does that?"

"That must have been hell for you," she said. "Poor baby."

I had pooped in a bucket when the head on my boat was broken. I had pooped in woods more than once, but those occasions were private ones. No one was watching, not even Brody. I'd committed all sorts of wrongs in my life. I'd suffered all sorts of humiliation, but pooping in public was where I drew the line. I'd make every effort to avoid having to face that unfortunate situation again.

Meanwhile, my brief stint as a prisoner had distracted Angelina and Brody from the effort to find the truth about Kate and Billy Buck. No progress had been made, and things were looking glum. I told Brody about my conversation with Angelina.

"What if we're wrong?" she asked.

"Then I don't know what else to do," I answered. "Our logic seems sound."

"I agree, but your little wrong turn with Pat Grant has me gun shy."

"What else is left to try?" I asked. "I can't be involved. You two haven't gotten anyone to talk. Someone gave us a false lead on Grant. The one girl who may know what happened changed her mind. The Chief is pressuring us for time. We're out of steps to take."

"I can't bring the girl in for questioning," she said. "Angelina will have to handle that."

"Work on her to get it done," I said. "Sorry for throwing a wrench in things."

"Rominger called me right away," she said. "Angelina called too. We were all worried about you."

"I appreciate your concern," I said. "I'm fine now, but my hands are tied as far as helping with this case."

"We'll regroup and get back to work," she said. "How are you going to spend your free time?"

"Go fishing," I said. "When in doubt, go fishing."

TWELVE

I got serious about the trout chasing that week. I went off the beaten path to some lightly fished streams and fished hard. I was rewarded with some quality brown trout and rainbows. I caught fat, chunky fish with brilliant colors against a beautiful mountain backdrop. I finally understood the allure of fishing for trout in the mountains. It was glorious. I felt no guilt for not assisting Angelina and Brody. I only had trout on my mind for a few days, plus I was staying out of trouble.

I also ran Red long and hard. We played the dirty sock game, chased Frisbees, and chewed through three tennis balls that week. He was ready if another mission called for his services. I even took a day to hike up to the plateau where Pop had grown his weed. I found a few little sprouts that may have been marijuana plants. I cleared the leaves and debris from around them and gave them some water, just in case.

I stood on the spot where I'd shot Cody Banner. I replayed that moment in my mind, seeing the bullet strike him in the back once again. I recalled the look on Brody's face when she realized what had just happened. I knew that it was a justified killing. I had no remorse for taking that man's life. I'd been more than lucky to escape without a murder charge, but I'd do it again if I had to.

I sat on a flat rock and tried to forgive myself for my sins. I'd come here for a new life. It was time for me to move on from my past. I couldn't go back and change it. I had Brody now, and a fresh start. My assault charge was only a bump in the road. There would probably be more, but I couldn't let that get me down. I had everything going for me otherwise, including a loving partner and a faithful dog. I looked up at the sky and took in its wonder. I gave a silent prayer of thanks. A lot had happened on that little flat spot near the top of the mountain. It now felt like a holy place. I made a mental note to come back and check on those little plants.

On my way down the mountain, I started thinking about Billy Buck's parents. Would knowing that he'd been drugged be enough to satisfy them? We could call it an accidental death rather than suicide. That was the original goal, to prove he didn't kill himself. We could talk to them and give it a try, but I doubted that it would be enough. They'd want to know the whole truth. I brought it up with Brody when I got home.

"We're past due for a visit with them anyway," she said. "We've gotten caught up in the investigating and forgotten the human factor."

"Call and ask if we can come over," I said. "Face to face is always best."

Brody made the call and arranged for us to see Darla and Frank the next day. We'd seen no additional payment from them, but we didn't bring it up. We didn't care about the money. We'd be willing to accept whatever they could afford, if anything.

We found them sitting in their rocking chairs on the porch when we pulled up. A pitcher of tea sat on the table between them. We each accepted a glass. It was sugary sweet like my great aunt used to make. Slices of lemon floated in the pitcher. It took me back to a simpler time.

"He didn't kill himself," Frank said. "Did he?"

"Someone drugged him," I said. "We don't know what happened after that. We suspect he had help falling off that spillway, but we can't prove it. It could have been an accident."

"Who do you suspect?" Darla asked.

"The girl he told you about," Brody said. "I'm sorry to say this, but we think his dates were part of a hoax. Some sorority ritual possibly."

"I don't understand," Darla said.

"You've heard of hazing?" I asked.

"Only vaguely," she answered. "They make kids do stupid stuff to get into the club."

"Kate was made to date Billy as part of her initiation," Brody said. "That's the theory anyway."

"Because he was different," Frank said. "He was a joke to them."

We didn't want to agree with that statement, so we didn't say anything. Silence hung over the porch like fog. I topped off my glass of tea and offered the pitcher to Brody. Frank got up and went inside. We sat in continued silence until he returned. He handed me a wad of bills.

"We'd like for you to prove who killed him," he said. "This is all we've got. If it turns out to have been an accident, we'll have to accept that. Be good to know who drugged him though. Can you do that for us, Breeze?"

"Brody is working with an Avery County deputy," I said. "I had a little trouble in Banner Elk, and I'm off the case."

"He roughed up a suspect," Brody said. "Spent the night in jail over it."

"Please don't resort to violence on account of us," Darla said.

"Sometimes that's what it takes," Frank said. "But getting yourself kicked off the case doesn't help our cause any."

"I apologize," I said. "But Brody and Deputy Will are quite capable."

"I thought the police were done with this," Frank said.

"When they discovered a date rape drug in his system their interest was renewed," I explained. "I convinced the Banner Elk Chief to reopen the case, but he's not much of an investigator. He called in one from the county to work with us."

"You know this fellow?"

"It's a she," I said. "And yes, we're quite familiar. We've worked together before."

"What's keeping you from getting at the truth?"

"Everyone is afraid to hurt the college's reputation," I said. "And the town's too. These things don't happen in Banner Elk."

"It happened to our boy," Frank said. "To hell with their reputations. The truth is all that matters."

Darla was visibly disturbed by Frank's little outburst. His fists were trembling at his side, and he had cursed. I thought he might want to punch a hole in something. Darla began to cry. I looked at Brody for help. I couldn't handle a woman crying. She went to Darla and held her in an extended hug. Frank stomped off to the barn, but I didn't follow. Their grief had not diminished, and we'd done nothing to help the process along. Brody helped Darla up and the two women went inside, leaving me alone on the porch. I sat and watched the sweat dribble down my glass. I heard Frank banging a hammer against metal down in the barn.

I was relieved when Brody returned, without Darla. She motioned with her eyes to the car. We left without speaking and drove away from the home of Frank and Darla Buck.

"I feel like we're letting them down," Brody said.

"Me too."

"What are we going to do, Breeze?" she asked.

"Solve the case," I said. "One way or another."

I counted out five-hundred dollars in cash that Frank had given me. I stuffed it in Brody's purse.

"Can't Angelina bring Kate in on reasonable suspicion?" I asked.

"An actual arrest calls for probable cause," she said. "Which is a higher bar, but all she has to do is exercise her right to remain silent. She'd lawyer up in a heartbeat."

"And without charges, we'd have to let her go," I said.

"I doubt she'll volunteer to sit and talk with the police," she said. "Even if we had cause to arrest her, she has a right to an attorney, the right against unlawful search, the right to keep her mouth shut. We've got nothing to arrest her on, except our suspicion."

"Somebody drugged the boy," I said. "She was with him the night it happened."

"So were others," she said. "None of whom are talking."

"What if we accused one of the other girls?" I said. "Make a big deal out of interrogating her. Wouldn't she spill the beans on Kate to defend herself?"

"You might be onto something," she said. "I need to check on our legal right to interrogate as private investigators. We may have a little more leeway than the cops do."

"Wish we could just kidnap one of them and waterboard her," I said.

"I'm pretty sure that's not within our rights," she said.

"Get me a list of Kate's sorority sisters that were at that party," I said. "I'll do a deep dive into their backgrounds and identify the weakest link."

"And then what?"

"You find out what's legal and what's not," I said. "I'll think of a way to get to our target individual and make her talk."

"I'm not sure I like where this is going?" she said.

"We've got to make something happen," I said. "For Frank and Darla's sake."

A plan was trying to formulate in my mind. It was devious and underhanded, but not outside the boundaries of my personal code of conduct. People in general were weak, some weaker than others. It had been my experience that today's college-aged kids were particularly fragile. Every tiny bit of friction triggered their sensibilities and sent them running to safe spaces, where they found solace from being offended. God forbid you express an opinion that was contrary to their worldview. I would find the weakest link in Kate's chain. I'd exploit that weak link until the whole thing fell apart.

We started with the list of names in Kate's inner circle. Brody began searching social media and public records for any interesting tidbits. I took it a step farther. I managed to talk Rominger into running background checks on each of the girls. I was looking for any arrests or domestic situations that I could use against them. The three of us worked the list for three days until we hit on our target. Rachel Marshall had been caught shoplifting when she was sixteen years old. She also had been arrested for possession of marijuana during her senior year of high school. Her Facebook and Instagram accounts painted her as a rebel. Some of her posts bordered on nudity. I'm sure her daddy would be proud. I could smell the psychological problems boiling under the surface with this girl. She attempted to portray toughness to hide her insecurities. She was the weak one.

We acquired her grades and her driving record. We knew that she had a car on campus and what make and model it was. Within three days we knew more about this girl than she knew about herself. Rachel's life was about to get uncomfortable. The vice would tighten slowly at first, but eventually, it would squeeze the truth out of her.

"What are we going to do with all of this information?" Brody asked.

"You'll see."

When I thought I had enough ammunition, I called for a meeting of the minds. I invited Angelina, Rominger and the Banner Elk Chief to our cabin to discuss my plan of action, and to enlist their help. Brody prepared some finger foods and offered beer and wine to each of our guests. It was our first experience at entertaining since we moved to North Carolina.

"The subject is Rachel Marshall," I began. "Nineteen-year-old female student at Lees-McRae. She's part of our main suspect's inner circle and a sorority sister. This team we've assembled is to embark on an intimidation campaign as part of a psychological angle to break down her defenses. Call it harassment if you like. We will pester her with her past misdeeds. We will write her traffic tickets for any minor infraction we can think of. We will pass her on the street and call her names."

"What's the end game?" asked Rominger.

"The finale is to accuse her of the murder of Billy Buck," I said. "But not until she's so rattled she can't think straight."

"But she didn't do it," Angelina said. "At least we don't think so."

"Doesn't matter," I said. "She'll give up the guilty party to save herself."

"It sounds good as a tactic," The Chief said. "But also skirts the edges of legality."

"We've got to be careful not to cross that line," I said. "Don't write her a ticket for something she didn't do. Write her a ticket for going twenty-seven in a twenty-five, or failing to use turn signals."

"What do we do with the rest of this stuff?" Angelina asked.

"It's going to take time and shoe leather," I began. "We need to be on her tail. On campus and in town. Down in Boone. Wherever she goes, we see her. We whisper *dope fiend* one time. We call her a shoplifter another time. We remind her how she failed geometry in the tenth grade. Eventually, we call her a killer. We walk by and say Billy Buck's name."

"And then?" the Chief asked.

"This is where it gets tricky," I said. "One of you cops has to pick her up, off the books. We take her somewhere and seriously interrogate her. She'll already be broken by this time. She won't ask for a lawyer, and if she does, we won't give her one. She tells us the whole story. We leave her sobbing in a dark room, promising to testify in court. We have to terrify her."

The three cops in the room looked at each other. I made eye contact with Brody and motioned for us to go outside. We retreated to the porch, letting our law enforcement friends decide how far they were willing to go.

"Do you think they'll agree to participate?" Brody asked.

"I say we get two out of three," I answered. "No guess as to which ones."

"It's a good plan," she said. "Aside from the questionable legality of your recommended approach."

"It's straight up harassment," I said. "I'd feel guilty if the girl wasn't complicit, but she knows what happened."

"I think you're right," she said. "At least enough for us to arrest Kate. We can build the case against her with a little help."

Rominger came to the door and called us back inside. We all took our seats around the table. I was curious as to who would take the lead among the three of them. I would have guessed Rominger, but it was Angelina who spoke first.

"It was almost unanimous," she said. "With one small catch. The three of us will participate in the campaign, but when it comes down to holding the girl for interrogation, Rominger is out."

"You on board, Chief?" I asked.

"I haven't done enough to help," he said. "It's a chance to finally end this thing."

"I'm agreeing because of my trust in you and Brody," Angelina said. "You've both become my good friends. I know that you're trying to do what's best. I also know that all our asses are going to be in a sling if we screw this up."

"I'll do what I can, Breeze," Rominger said. "But I'm bucking for a promotion. Now is not a good time for stepping out of bounds. I can help up to that point."

"Fair enough," I said. "I want to thank all three of you. We made copies so each of you can have a file. We've got pictures of her and her car. We've got her class schedule. We know what hairdresser she uses. We know what bars she likes."

"If you can make contact with her while on duty that's great, but don't get yourselves in a bind at work," Brody said. "Off duty is even better when you can swing it."

"My whole force can watch for her in town," the Chief said. "How many tickets you want her to get?"

"Only legit ones," I said. "But as petty as you want to be."

"I'll bust the bitch for jaywalking," he said.

"We've all got to stay in touch," Brody explained. "Let the rest know where she is and what she's doing whenever possible."

"I've got to hand it to you, Breeze," said the Chief. "This is thinking outside the box."

"It's unconventional," I admitted. "But think of it as bypassing the fortified gate and sneaking in the side door. We're finding a spot that's not heavily defended. Once inside, we can kill the queen."

"Should we swear a secret oath or something?" asked Angelina.

"Let's bring her down," I said.

"Bring her down," said Brody.

"Bring her down," said the others.

Thirteen

The Chief distributed a picture of Rachel's car along with her license plate number to all of his officers in Banner Elk. One of them caught her doing four miles per hour over the speed limit on Main Street in front of Dunn's Deli. He wrote her a warning and told her she wouldn't be so lucky the next time. She whined about it that night on Facebook, calling the cops stupid. This was a big mistake on her part. A few days later, another officer clocked her at forty-one in a thirty-five zone. She got a speeding ticket from a less than friendly cop. Again she took to Facebook to complain.

Brody and Angelina took turns stalking the campus and keeping an eye out for Rachel. They even went so far as to pay other students to whisper things to the girl in passing. The college kids were happy to take twenty bucks to say *shoplifter* to her and keep on walking. I stayed off campus but nearby. I'd get a call whenever she got in her car to go someplace. I'd pick up her tail and call an officer on duty to report her location and direction of travel. If she left the town limits of Banner Elk, I'd call Rominger so he could alert his Highway Patrol buddies. They'd also been told about Rachel's distaste for police officers and had no compunction about pulling her over for minor offenses. It didn't take long for one of them to bust her for failing to signal on her way to Boone.

She had two tickets and a warning in the first week of our campaign. Brody, Angelina, and random students had called her various names on campus and the streets of the town. The names turned to vague accusations during the second week. *I know what you did. You should be ashamed.* One night she went to a bar in Blowing Rock. We knew her to be nineteen, not old enough to legally purchase alcohol. Rominger called the Blowing Rock PD and had them raid the bar. Rachel was caught up in the fake ID sweep as a result. The bar owner was let off the hook, but Rachel was not. Her car was impounded, and she was delivered to the police station for an intimidation session. She was threatened with the loss of her license for one year and a fine of up to one-thousand dollars. After consultation with Rominger, who relayed to me, we all decided not to pursue those charges that would prevent her from driving. We weren't done with her yet. Instead, she was charged with unlawful purchase of alcohol by an underage person. This amounted to a slap on the wrist.

There were costs involved in getting her car back, which proved to be a hardship for her. She was held up at the police station until it was too late to free the vehicle that night. Rominger had a Highway Patrol officer take her back to Lees-McRae. She got a ride back to Blowing Rock the next day to retrieve her car. I followed her both ways, noticing how she never exceeded the speed limit and always used her turn signals on the way home. Angelina was waiting outside her dorm when she returned.

"Rough night, I hear," she said. "Not as rough as Billy Buck."

"What are you talking about?" the girl asked.

"Billy's dead," Angelina replied, before walking away.

We gave her a few days to recover before we resumed our tactics. We disappeared again after two days. Cops followed her everywhere, but she didn't do a thing that would warrant a ticket. One night she posted on Facebook that this hick-ass little town was driving her crazy. We changed our passing mutterings to *killer* and *murderer*. Several of the participating policemen called her phone and used the same words before hanging up. We pushed her to the limits of sanity. It was time for the coup de grace, but we were all nervous about it. We planned to kidnap the girl, after all. It wasn't an assignment that any cop would take lightly. I huddled with the team again at our cabin.

"I don't have a problem with going in and snatching her," I said. "But it's only been a few weeks since I spent the night in jail. I may not be the best candidate."

"Me neither," said Rominger. "This is where I step back."

We all looked at Angelina and the Chief. Brody got a notification on her phone and looked at it.

"New post from our little friend," she said, showing me the phone.

"Stupid, fucking, dumb ass, cops. I swear they've got it in for me," I read aloud.

"Let me see that," said the Chief. "Sumbitch. Let me take a picture of this."

He messaged the screenshot to his men on the police force. He got several quick replies that we weren't privy to.

"Let me call a meeting down at the station," he said. "I reckon I can get some volunteers."

"You've got to be upfront with them," I said. "This is not an official arrest. We're taking her against her will and accusing her of something we don't think she did."

"They'll understand," he said. "But it's more people in on our conspiracy."

"It's an effort to get the truth," Brody pointed out. "We want her to testify against Kate."

"Are we absolutely positive that Kate killed Billy Buck?" the Chief asked.

Brody and I hesitated. We were not one-hundred percent sure that Kate had killed Billy. We strongly believed that her actions led to his death, but we couldn't say that she shoved him off that spillway.

"We are not positive that she killed him," Brody said. "We are positive that she knows what happened. Whether it was an accident or not. We're fairly sure that Kate or one of her sorority sisters drugged him, but we have no proof. We need Rachel to tell us what went down. That's the whole point."

"And we selected this individual on what basis?" he asked.

"It's a little late to get cold feet now, Chief," I said. "I determined that she was the weakest, and therefore the most likely to break ranks. Brody agreed."

"I assume you have some experience in this type of profiling?"

"I know people," I said. "Especially those on the fringes. My life has depended on making quick judgments as to character. Brody did the same thing at the Bureau."

"I knew there was a reason I wanted your help on this case," he said. "Something told me you knew how to get shit done."

"We should add that to our business cards," I said.

"Give me a day," he said. "I'll let you know if my men want a piece of this. It will look legit with uniformed officers picking her up. No offense Angelina, but big, strong men are much more intimidating."

"No offense taken," Angelina said. "But I'll grab her if your men don't want to volunteer."

"Noted," the Chief said. "You've got a certain moxie too."

"I'll take that as a compliment," Angelina said.

"The ball's rolling downhill too fast to stop it now," the Chief said. "I'll call all of you tomorrow."

Rominger and the Chief left. Angelina remained. Brody made a pot of coffee. The three of us sat at the dining room table and shared a few moments of quiet.

"This is a nice place," Angelina said. "Just the right amount of rustic and comfort."

"We've tried to make it comfortable," Brody said.

"So why do you two do this stuff?" she asked. "Cute little cabin. Just the two of you alone in the woods. Why get involved in high drama?"

"Good question," Brody answered. "It's a Breeze thing."

"Don't let her fool you," I said. "She needs a little action fix now and then too. She's been more involved in this one than I have."

"I think I could learn to live with the solitude," Angelina said. "Seems better than chasing mountain hermits and meth-heads to me."

"We were enjoying it," I said. "It was Billy's parents that drew us in."

"I forgot about that," she said. "How are they doing?"

"They're not going to let it go until we reach a final conclusion," I said. "They gave us what is probably their life savings to get us to continue."

"Billy's mom cried on my shoulder," Brody told her. "I couldn't say no."

"His father is still angry," I said. "Anger doesn't become him, but I can't blame him."

"We're close," Angelina said. "We'll shake it out of this girl. She's all set up."

"I think so too," I said. "She'll sing an entire opera as soon as we lay hands on her."

"I hope you two are right," Brody said.

"Doubts?" I asked.

"What's keeping Rachel from exposing our scheme?"

"She's going to appear unstable if she starts spouting off conspiracy theories," I said.

"Won't that cause questions about her testimony?"

"We will make it clear that there will be consequences if she doesn't cooperate," I said.

"She knows we can get to her anytime we want," Angelina said.

"I might disappear if it was me," Brody said.

"Then we keep her under surveillance," I said. "We can't let her slip away now."

"We're only a few people," she said.

"Let's put a tracker on her car," Angelina said. "It's a simple thing to do."

"Can you arrange that?" I asked.

"I'll have it done while she's in custody," she replied. "We'll know where the car is at all times."

"I like it," I said. "Does that make you feel any better, Brody?"

"A little," she said. "I'm just nervous I guess."

"You had to have some pretty hairy situations with the FBI," I said. "This should be child's play."

"Don't tell me you never skirted the law working with them," Angelina said.

"We did," Brody said. "Too many times, but we had that badge to back us up."

"Okay, so the Banner Elk PD isn't the FBI," I said. "But we've got three agencies involved in this. I think our asses are covered."

"You two are amazing," Angelina said. "Out of nowhere, you've got law enforcement wrapped around your finger, conspiring together to break a case, in all sorts of illegal ways."

"We found people like us," I said. "People who want justice, no matter what it takes."

"Angelina Will," she said. "In search of truth, justice, and the American Way."

"Some things are worth stretching the boundaries for," I said.

"I guess we've all decided this is one of those times," Brody said.

"For Frank and Darla," I said.

"And Billy," Brody said.

"Bring her down," said Angelina.

We touched our coffee mugs like we were making a toast with champagne. As soon as Angelina, left I traded the coffee for Tennessee Whiskey. I wouldn't be able to sleep without taking the edge off. Brody went out and sat in her rocking chair on the porch. I could hear the katydids singing while the door was open. I sat and sipped my liquor for a few minutes before joining her. I reached out to hold her hand as we rocked together, listening to the song of the woods and the unending murmur of the creek. It started to rain lightly. The drops tapped on our tin roof, adding to the symphony. It was one of those moments that made living in the mountains special.

"I love you, Brody."

"Just tell me this is going to work out for the best," she said.

"It's going to be okay," I said. "We're on the side of good here."

"Is that your gut talking?"

"My gut says full steam ahead," I said. "No worries."

"That's good," she said. "That's a good thing."

There had been no recent contact with our main suspect, Kate. As far as we could tell, Rachel had not gone to visit her either. Since her ill-fated trip to Blowing Rock, she hadn't gone anywhere or been spotted with friends. We'd turned her into an island. Even surrounded by fellow students, she was alone. The Chief called with news that two of his officers were willing to participate in our scheme. They were ready when we were. Rominger was out, so I didn't need to call him. Brody called Angelina. We agreed on the following night to swing into action. The last phase of the mission would soon be underway.

Brody paced incessantly while chewing on her fingernails. It was uncommon for her to be so nervous. I knew something about our planning was still bothering her.

"Come out with it," I said.

"We've harassed Rachel to the breaking point," she said. "I get that, but we can't predict how she's going to react."

"What can she do?" I asked. "Take the rap for Billy's murder? Run?"

"I don't know," she said. "She seemed potentially unstable before we set out to destroy her psyche. Now she's a tight wire, ready to snap."

"We're about to give her a way out," I said. "We're offering her peace of mind as long as she turns on Kate. She'll be grateful."

"Angelina better make sure we get a GPS tracker on her car," she said. "If she gives us what we want, she becomes real valuable to us. We've put all our eggs in this basket. We lose her, and the jig is up."

"Anything else that can go wrong?"

"She could freak out on the cops who pick her up," she said. "Kick and scream and raise holy hell. We don't want them to hurt her, and we don't need the whole world seeing her taken into custody."

"I'll bring it up with the Chief," I said. "I still don't know where they are taking her."

"Find out," she said. "We've got to cover every detail."

I called the Chief to find out where his men were taking the girl. Next to the police station was a small strip mall of sorts that housed a brewery and a metal works. One of the units was unoccupied. He'd put a few folding chairs and a table inside. The power was on. I knew where he was talking about. He thought that it would look natural to have the patrol cars pull into their normal spots, we just wouldn't take the girl into the station. It would happen after dark. He instructed us to park behind the facility.

Brody and I drove down the mountain to check it out. It took us a minute to figure out which door led to the vacant unit. We called Angelina and agreed to meet behind the strip mall at seven. We went to the Banner Elk Café for a pizza. The staff looked like the same kids we'd seen before. Every employee had a phone in their pocket or their hand. They were pleasant enough, but none seemed very serious about providing excellent service. They managed to do what was required, and that was about it. On the other hand, the place was clean, and the pizza was good. We left an ample tip and drove home to wait for zero-hour.

We both grew impatient, so we left a little early. Angelina was already waiting for us when we arrived. The Chief showed up soon after and let us in the back door. The inside was bare of furnishings except for the folding chairs and table.

"I took the liberty of hanging that lone bulb from the rafters," the Chief said. "It's one-hundred watts, biggest I could find."

"Adds to the ambiance," I said. "Not that different from a movie set torture room."

"That's what I was going for," he said. "Two big goons bring her in and sit her in that chair. The three of us tag team her with questions. She'll be frightened and confused."

"We need to be careful not to lead her with our questions," Brody said. "Don't tell her we think Kate is responsible. Remember, we tell her that we think she did it. Let her tell us about Kate of her own free will."

"We all accuse her," Angelina said. "One by one we tell her she's guilty of murder and she's in a lot of trouble. Her life is over."

"She'll have no choice but to tell us the truth," I said. "That's the plan, anyway."

"If it leads us somewhere else?" Brody asked.

"We stay quick on our feet," I said. "Improvise. Learn everything she knows."

"Don't forget to dangle the carrot," Angelina said. "She not only goes free, but the harassment stops, as long as she's honest with us."

"With the understanding that if she's not honest, it won't go well for her," I added.

"We're all on the same page," the Chief said. "Let me call my boys."

It was barely past sunset so they wouldn't move immediately. They decided to wait for another hour. They had helpers keeping an eye on her dorm exits. The pickup team would be alerted if she left the building. An hour crawled by with no one having much to say. When the Chief's phone rang it startled all of us. The mission was underway. They'd be here with the girl soon. The Chief went to the back door and propped it open. Angelina,

Brody, and I took a seat in front of the table. There was one chair left across from us for Rachel.

Two big cops held Rachel between them by the arms. She walked stiffly with no expression. They motioned for her to sit. She scooted her chair up and rested her arms on the table.

"Someone want to tell me what this is all about?" she said.

"It's about murder," Angelina said, getting up from her chair. "You killed Billy Buck."

"I had nothing to do with it," Rachel said. "You're wrong."

"We know you did it," Brody said. "You're going to go away for a long time."

"I didn't kill him," she said, starting to sob.

"Make it easy on yourself," I told her. "Confess and plead guilty. That might save you ten years or so."

"Why are you doing this to me?" she asked. "I didn't hurt anybody. I'm not a killer."

Angelina stood over our captive, invading her personal space. She tapped a black baton on her palm, threatening violence.

"You think you're better than people like Billy," she said. "That his life doesn't matter. We're about to get some payback for what you did to him."

Brody got up and eased Angelina away from the table.

"We just want the truth," Brody said. "All you have to do is tell us what happened that night."

Rachel burst into a bawling fit. She put her head in her hands and cried loudly and long. Real tears ran down her face. She was broken. I looked at the two women. Brody pointed to her chest. She was taking it from here.

She comforted the crying girl like only a woman can do. Rachel put her head on Brody's shoulder, her bawling reduced to a whimper. Brody stroked her hair and told her that everything was going to be all right. When the girl began to compose herself, Brody led her in the direction we needed to go.

"Tell us what happened," Brody said. "If you didn't kill Billy, who did?"

"I didn't kill him," she said. "I didn't see what happened to him. I left and went back to my room. The next day he was dead. He was alive when I left."

"Who slipped him a mickey?" Brody asked. "Who drugged him?"

"That was Kate," she said.

"Why did Kate give Billy drugs?"

"She was supposed to have sex with him, and she didn't want him to remember," Rachel said.

"Why?"

"Sorority pledge challenge," she said.

"So you saw him under the influence," Brody said. "How did he act?"

"He didn't know where he was," she said. "He couldn't stand on his own."

"Who else saw him in that condition?"

"There were four or five of us," she said. "They all thought it was funny."

"Why did everyone leave with him in that state?"

"I told you," she said. "Kate had to have sex with him. There was a camera and a microphone set up. That was the deal."

"Did she do it?"

"The video was inconclusive as far as I could tell," she said. "Kate turned off the lights. Billy was out of it on the bed."

"How did he get to the spillway if he couldn't walk?"

"Kate had to take him," she said. "But I didn't see it happen."

"After the alleged sex took place, what else was on the video?"

"Kate taking Billy out of the frame," she said. "That was it."

"Kate physically helped him to his feet?"

"She practically carried him to the door," Rachel said. "If he had sex that night, he sure didn't know it."

I saw something in her body language; this wasn't the whole truth. She was leaving something out. What she'd told us was accurate, but there was more to the story. She was calculating that it was enough for us to leave her alone. The crying had been real, but she'd recovered enough to continue to withhold the whole truth.

Fourteen

I got up from my chair, walked over to the flimsy table and kicked it across the room. I stood in front of Rachel, bending down to put my face inches from hers. I stared at her for a minute, causing her to look away.

"What's the rest of the story?" I yelled in her face. "Spit it out before I lose my patience. Now!"

She cringed and tried to put some space between us. I used a foot to sweep the chair out from under her. She fell awkwardly backward. I knelt beside her and grabbed her up by the front of her shirt.

"This ain't no high school glee club, you little shit," I said. "Not a sorority tea party either. You will talk."

"Okay, okay," she said. "Please, don't hurt me."

"Better tell him what else you know," Brody said. "Did you hear what he did to Pat Grant?"

"I didn't see it happen," she said. "But Kate killed him."

"How do you know if you didn't see it?" I asked.

"She told us."

I pulled her to her feet and gave her back the chair. Angelina came over and nudged me out of the way. I was happy for her to take over.

"She admitted killing Billy?" Angelina asked the girl.

"We all met in her room the next day to watch the video," she began. "Everyone knew that he was dead by then. We pushed her about it. She made us take some silly sorority oath of silence before she would tell."

"What did she tell you?"

"That she led him down the path to the millpond," Rachel said. "Made him walk the plank."

"She saw him fall?"

"Yes," she said. "She laughed about it. Said he was too dumb and disgusting to live."

"She admitted that the fall could kill him?" Angelina asked. "It's not that far of a drop."

"She saw him hit the rocks hard," she said. "He could barely walk as it was. No way he could make it over the top of the dam."

"Why would she admit to murder?"

"She thought it was the most epic pledge challenge in the history of Lees-McRae," she said. "She'd be a sorority legend."

"And no one would talk about it because of your oath of silence?"

"That's right," she said. "All the girls knew about it sooner or later. The entire sorority was sworn to silence."

"Do you realize that makes you an accessory after the fact?"

"I had nothing to do with Billy's death," she said. "I keep telling you that."

"Protecting the killer is a crime," I said. "You should have gone to the police immediately."

"Whatever sentence Kate gets for murder," the Chief said. "You'll get half. You can expect a minimum of fifteen years."

"But I didn't do anything," she said.

"We're not making this up," Angelina told her. "You're in deep shit."

"But I didn't know," she said, tears starting to flow again. "I can't go to jail."

Brody went to the girl and handed her a handkerchief. She placed one hand gently on her shoulder.

"We can get you out of this," Brody said. "Give us a written statement and agree to testify against Kate, and this will all go away."

"I'll have to check with the lawyers on that," said the Chief.

"You tell the lawyers that we made this deal in good faith," Brody said. "What's it going to be Rachel?"

"I'll do it," she said. "Tell me what to do."

Looks of satisfaction were shared around the room. The chief had his two officers escort the girl over to the police station. He called someone at the District Attorney's office. Rachel was put in a cell while we all waited for a lawyer to arrive. She never once asked for a lawyer of her own. She was given a soda and a snack before everyone left her alone. We sat in the Chief's office to wait.

"Is it enough?" Brody asked.

"It's not hearsay because it didn't come from a third person," Angelina said. "It came from the mouth of the killer."

"We are the third person," Brody said. "We are taking the word of the second person."

"Who heard it directly from the first person," Angelina came back. "Now that we've broken one of them, it shouldn't be hard to get more of the girls to corroborate her testimony."

"We've got grounds to call all of them in for official questioning," The Chief said. "Rachel has implicated them."

"We threaten them all with accessory," Angelina said. "They'll cave one by one. By the time it gets to court we'll have a dozen girls all saying the same thing."

"Which will be more than enough," I said. "Kate's going down."

That got a smile out of everyone, even Brody. Hugs were exchanged, and the mood lightened considerably. We'd been beating our heads against the wall trying to break this case; now it looked like our efforts would be rewarded. I was ready to go home, but Brody wanted to stay and see it through. The DA's office was sending a low-level employee to witness the willing written statement by Rachel. They had no idea what was involved in acquiring her cooperation. Angelina and Brody would guide them through the process. We'd have the document in hand, which would lead to Kate's arrest and eventual conviction.

I asked Angelina to verify that a GPS tracker had been placed on Rachel's car. The answer was affirmative. I tried to think of anything else we might have missed. That answer was negative. I excused myself long enough to drive to Food Lion for a six-pack of beer. I sat in the police station parking lot and popped a cold one. Brody came out to check on me, and I offered one to her.

"You're a genius," she said. "Just what I needed right now."

We clinked our cans together in a tiny display of celebration. This case would instantly elevate the reputation of Creekside Investigations. We could pick and choose our jobs from here on out.

"Nice work, former G-man," I told Brody.

"The credit goes to you," she said. "I'm not devious enough to devise a plan like that."

"It worked, didn't it?"

"Thanks to a team effort," she said. "But let's face it; you were the brains behind this operation."

"I'm still not sure that's a compliment."

"Let's make sure this all holds together before we celebrate too much," she said. "We're a long way from a guilty verdict."

"I wish I could be part of the jury selection process," I said. "We need salt of the earth types, farmers, loggers, and hunters. I'd keep every academic off that jury."

"You think the locals will have sympathy for Kate?"

"They will still want to protect the college," I said. "And the reputation of the town. I'd hold the trial down in Newland. Pull my jury from that area."

"Maybe we should be trial consultants too," she said. "You seem to have a handle on it."

"No legal background for either of us," I said. "It would be tough to convince potential clients to give us a chance."

"Then we stick to what we know," she said. "But add *we get shit done* to our literature."

"And hound dog for hire," I added. "A multi-faceted investigative enterprise."

"Our business card is getting a little crowded."

"We'll have all the work we want after this business is finished," I said. "Word will get around."

We finished our beers and returned to the Chief's office. The lawyer showed up soon after. We spent a few minutes bringing him up to speed before he was taken in to see Rachel. She seemed almost glad to see him. He asked her a few questions first.

"Are you providing this written statement of your own free will?"

"Yes sir, I am," she said.

"You are not under arrest," he said. "But you are entitled to a lawyer if you so choose."

"I don't need a lawyer," she said.

"Do you swear that what you're about to offer is the whole truth and nothing but the truth?"

"I do," she answered.

"There is a section of this document that explains any false statement by you is punishable by the law," he said. "Do you understand that?"

"Yes, I understand."

She wrote down her testimony with the lawyer's help. He showed her where to sign the documents. He was satisfied that he had what he needed, but made clear that we needed to sit down with the DA before proceeding any further. The whole county would have an interest in these proceedings, so every detail had to be accounted for. We all acknowledged his advice and agreed to cooperate fully with the DA's office.

Rachel was free to go. Angelina offered to drive her back to campus. That meant that Brody and I were free as well. We shook hands with the Chief before leaving the station.

"Pleasure working with you two," he said. "I'll be sure to call on you when the situation warrants."

"Thanks, Chief," Brody said. "Breeze isn't so bad once you get to know him."

"I'm starting to realize that," he said. "Go on and take it easy now. I'll keep you up to date as the case moves forward."

"Good to work with you," I said. "I appreciate the leeway you've given us."

"It wouldn't have gotten done without it," he said. "Works that way sometimes."

"Take care, Chief."

"One last thing," he said. "Stay away from campus. Let us take it from here. Lay low until this is wrapped up."

"I could use a little fishing time anyway," I said. "We've done our part."

There was a meeting at the District Attorney's Office down in Bakersville the next day. We weren't invited, but Angelina filled us in. Brody and I were to keep quiet about our involvement until the suspect was in custody. The DA listened to her, and the Chief put the case together. He read Rachel's written statement and gave the greenlight for Kate's arrest. She would be charged with second-degree murder, meaning it was intentional but not premeditated. A judge would determine if she could post bail or not. The DA would push for one million dollars if he thought the judge was inclined to grant bail. Two Banner Elk police officers were dispatched to pick up the alleged murderer.

We waited for word that she was behind bars, but it didn't come. I called the Chief after dinner to find out what was going on.

"We haven't found her yet," he said. "She's not in her dorm room, and her car isn't on campus."

"We should have put the tracker on her car," I said.

"You think she's in the wind?" he asked. "She didn't know we were coming for her."

"Rachel may have alerted her," I said. "She could have told her last night after we cut her loose."

"Shit," the Chief said. "You could be right. I'll go drill Rachel right now."

"If she informed Kate, she should lose all the leniency that we offered her," I said. "Lock her ass up."

"This thing went to hell quickly," he said.

"If she's on the run it's blown to bits until we find her," I said. "Put out an APB or whatever it is you do. All hands on deck."

"I want you to stay home," he said. "Help us with some research. Her parent's address, likely haunts, friends, and relatives."

"We're on it," I said. "We'll call with anything pertinent."

"Fuck me running," he said. "Damn, damn, and damn."

"You'll find her," I said. "Get busy."

Angelina called a few minutes later. The Chief had alerted all neighboring agencies. All available staff was on the street looking for Kate's car, a late model silver Honda Civic. At least it wasn't a white Subaru. There were thousands of those on the roads in the area. As soon as she hung up, Rominger called. Highway Patrol wanted her parents' address if they lived in North Carolina. Brody was working on it. I promised to call back.

That's how the rest of the night went. Brody worked some computer magic to learn the intimate life details of one Katherine Leslie as we'd done with Rachel. Her driver's license listed her home address in a suburb of Charlotte. We soon learned the workplaces of both the mother and father. Dad's company owned a beach house on Nags Head. Highway patrol sent cars to each location. A call was made to her parent's house, but it went unanswered. We continued searching and coordinating with law enforcement until the wee hours of the morning. Kate had not returned to her dorm room. Her car had not been spotted. She was gone.

"I'm calling the FBI," Brody said. "They have the technology to locate her."

"Your old boyfriend told us we'd get no help from him," I reminded her. "We no longer exist to them."

"This is not about us," she said. "It's about helping local law enforcement with a manhunt. They do it all the time."

"Make the call," I said. "Good luck."

I listened as Brody spoke to an old friend at the Bureau. The agent agreed to forward her request higher up the chain. We got a call back within the hour. Brody answered all their questions, giving them the information they needed to get started. Within minutes, the FBI accessed her bank account and credit card information. License plates readers were programmed to sound the alarm if she was spotted on any highway in the country. If she used her cards to get cash or pay for gas, the FBI would know about it. Her location could be pinpointed immediately in any number of ways. A description of her car along with the tag number was distributed nationwide. A naïve teenage girl was no match for the sophisticated technology that the FBI could employ. Not even savvy adult criminals could hide for long. Modern society had created Big Brother for just this type of situation. Cameras were everywhere. We assumed she would be found at any minute.

I manned the phones while Brody got some sleep. We switched places around noon. Kate had still not been located. I slept until four, fully expecting to hear good news when I woke up. There was no news.

"How can this be happening?" I asked. "How can she just disappear?"

"She had to get someplace before the search began in earnest," she said. "And she got there without using a credit or debit card."

"So she's within a tank full of gas from here," I said. "Check the range of a Honda Civic."

"It's five hundred miles," she said.

Brody pulled up Google Maps and drew a big circle. It covered a shocking amount of territory, including Washington, Indianapolis, Nashville, and even northern Florida.

"She could be anywhere," I said.

"She could have bought gas with cash," Brody added. "That makes the circle twice as big."

"One of those electronic methods will spot her sooner or later," I said. "She has to come up for air."

"She's not on an interstate, or we'd have her already," Brody said. "I still say she's holed up, and not too far away, unless she was able to change cars."

"You think she's that smart?"

"It's what I'd do if I were a murderer on the run," she said. "Ditch that car, take a friend's or relatives', stay on the back roads and spend only cash."

"We need cops to drive by the homes of everyone she knows," I said.

"Tall order," she said. "But I'll start working on a list."

"We need them to revisit the parents' places over and over again."

"Her car will be found," she said. "That will at least give us a lead. We have to be patient."

"It should have been found by now," I said. "I don't picture her hiding in some backcountry holler."

"Me neither," she said. "She wouldn't demean herself that way. She's someplace comfortable."

"I'm having a hard time trying to think like a teenage girl," I said. "I'm going to take Red outside for a bit. Get some air."

Red came to attention at the mention of his name. I let him out the door, and he took off running around the yard. He made two laps before picking up a tennis ball and dropping it at my feet. I threw if for him, marveling at the simplicity of his life. He didn't need much to make him happy. I gave him a warm place to sleep, good food, and plenty of exercise. Other than the occasional mission to use the skills he was born with, that's all he required.

I wished that our fugitive was hiding in the woods, and Red and I got a chance to track her down. That's what we were good at. All this computer stuff was not to our liking.

I tried to break down the problem into its simplest components. The girl had been given a head start, thanks to Rachel. She'd gotten somewhere quick and ditched her car. Maybe she now had a different car, maybe not. She was young and pampered, not well prepared to evade a dragnet like the one that had been set up for her, yet she still hadn't been found. Someone had to be helping her, but who? I was considering a sorority connection when Brody waved for me to come back inside. There was news.

Kate's car had been found at the Tri-Cities Airport in Tennessee. That was only sixty miles from Banner Elk. Surveillance tapes had been reviewed that showed her entering the parking garage the same night we'd taken Rachel. Rachel was now in custody again, having admitted that she'd warned Kate as soon as she returned to campus. The airport would accept cash for a ticket, but valid ID was required.

"Rachel had a fake ID," I said. "It was a pretty good one. Maybe Kate has one too."

"They're going back through the tapes at the ticket counters," Brody said. "It's tedious work."

"Could be a ruse," I said. "Criminals leave cars at the airport hoping it will be a while before someone notices. Doesn't have to mean she got a flight."

"Someone could have picked her up," Brody said.

"Ask the FBI to get into her phone," I said. "If they haven't already."

Brody made a call. The news wasn't good. Kate's phone was left in her car, turned off. She had made a few calls earlier that night. A tech was working on identifying those numbers.

"One of the people she called could have picked her up, given her another car, or knows where she was heading," Brody said.

"And given her cash," I offered. "But who and why? She's a stone cold killer."

"They wouldn't know that," she said. "She's still auntie's sweet little angel, or whatever."

"So we wait," I said.

"Nothing else we can do."

FIFTEEN

Brody's FBI contact called the next day with some interesting information. Kate's father had a company registered in Delaware. It wasn't a brick and mortar business, just a post office box. He used it to hide some off the books transactions from the eyes of auditors, and possibly the IRS. The key finding was that there were several phone numbers connected to the front business. One of them was called by Kate the night she disappeared. It last pinged a tower in Bristol, Tennessee. The other phone was in the possession of Kate's father. Its last known activity was in Charlotte, North Carolina, on the same night. Neither of the phones contacted the other.

Kate's parents had shown up at the beach house in Nags Head. Highway Patrol had spoken with them. They claimed no knowledge of her disappearance. They hadn't heard from her in a few days. They were informed that their daughter was the subject of a nationwide manhunt. They were not told that their phones and devices were all being monitored for contact with Kate. They weren't told about the company phone being located either. The trooper who spoke to them didn't know the details of the case, which was just as well.

We could make an educated guess that someone connected to the father or his business had picked up Kate from Tri-Cities Airport. Bristol was only twenty minutes north. The fact that she had otherwise avoided the awesome surveillance capabilities of the FBI was suspicious in itself. She wouldn't be able to pull that off on her own. We needed to know who had that phone. The father would have to tell us.

Meanwhile, Brody and I no longer had any official connection to the case. We'd been asked to lay low until it was resolved. It would never be concluded if we couldn't find the missing girl, though.

"Who is going to hire us as consultants on this?" I asked Brody. "We've got to be involved in finding her."

"If you want to drive to Nags Head it would have to be Highway Patrol," she answered. "Call Rominger."

I explained to my cop friend that we had unlimited time to devote to the slightest lead. We were free to travel, and we had a vested interest. We'd do it for free if it came to that, we just needed permission to participate. He said he would consult with his boss and get back to me.

"Brainstorm it," I said. "Who has that phone?"

"Business partner, employee, family member," Brody said.

"Someone very close and trusted," I added. "But who hasn't called Kate's father."

"He could have called him from a different phone," she said. "These company phones appear to be for special occasions only."

"Get somebody to run daddy's call record since she disappeared," I said. "Maybe there's a clue in there somewhere."

"Sounds like daddy didn't even know she was missing," she said.

"That's what he told the officer," I said. "Doesn't mean it's true. We need to question him face to face."

Brody called the FBI. While she was on the phone, Rominger called me back.

"Bossman says if I hold your hand you can help," he said. "But I've got to keep you out of trouble, or it's my ass on the line."

"Is that acceptable to you?"

"It would be if I knew you wouldn't cross the line," he said.

"Let's start with a trip to the coast," I said. "I need to meet with the girl's father."

"Nags Head?"

"That's where he is," I said. "You've got the run of the state don't you?"

"Normally we stay within our assigned district," he said. "But technically we're authorized anywhere in North Carolina. I'll need to call the boys at the shore to let them know I'm on their turf."

"Do it," I said. "Then tell me when you're ready to roll."

"Call you back."

Brody got on the computer to retrieve a call log sent by the FBI. Each number was tagged with the name associated with that account. There were a dozen different numbers on the list.

"Where do we start?" I asked.

"We find out who these people are and what their connection is," she said.

"I don't think I'll be much help," I said.

"Step aside mountain man," she said. "I, unlike you, am no Luddite."

I was indeed averse to modern technology, even as I witnessed what it could do. It could be me that Big Brother was tracking down. Hell, it had been me at one time. The reason that they couldn't find me is that I had no phone or computer. I had no credit cards or bank account. I lived on a boat and preferred secret coves to crowded beaches. I didn't own a car or even a driver's license back then. They were stumped. Staying offline is what kept me a free man. I'd evolved only recently to accept the phones and computers that we now had. We needed them to survive in the modern world, at least that's what Brody told me. I could have done without them forever, but not if we wanted to run a business. I wasn't wanted by the law these days; I was helping the law. My only worry, and it was a small one, was that one of the bad guys would track me down.

I didn't have a good case for this worry. It wasn't logical that my enemies would waste their time on me now. As more and more time passed, I should worry less, but staying alert for the possibility could mean the difference between life and death. Our accounts were under the business name, but I knew that a skilled researcher could figure out who was behind Creekside Investigations. The hope was that our little business would never be on anyone's radar. Still, it was a big concession for me to give in to phones and computers.

Brody was hammering away at the keyboard. I could see multiple tabs open on her browser. She was good at this sort of thing. She enjoyed it even. I was good at sneaking about the woods. I was good with my dog. I was in touch with the earth but still hopelessly ignorant to the internet. I didn't see that changing anytime soon. If something were to happen to Brody, I'd toss all of those devices in a dumpster and disappear into the wilderness.

I took Red out back for a while and let him do his thing. He marked his favorite trees while we walked the perimeter of the yard. He acted like he wanted to go up the mountain, but I didn't have time for a hike. He pulled a long lost Frisbee out of the weeds at the edge of the woods and brought it to me excitedly. I flung it back towards the house and watched him run. The yard sloped downward to the cabin. The spinning disc caught an updraft and carried impossibly far. It must have traveled a hundred yards before finally settling down in the driveway. Even Red was impressed. I raised my hands in the air and made fake crowd roaring noises. Breeze comes out of nowhere and breaks the all-time Frisbee distance record.

Brody appeared at the door and called us both back inside.

"Pretty good toss for an old man," she said.

"Meet me in the bedroom," I said. "I'll show you old."

"Later maybe," she said. "Help me with this list."

I pulled a chair up to the computer desk, not knowing what I was looking for.

"I've eliminated half the names," she said. "No connection to the family or the business. Hardware store, pizza delivery and the like."

"What do you have on the rest of them?"

"Not much, yet," she said. "I need to prioritize them. I'll get the FBI to give me the scoop on the important ones."

"What's our criteria?"

"Frequency of contact, connection to others on the list," she said. "Who's important out of these six?"

"What else do you have for me to go on?"

She clicked me through the other tabs and explained what they meant. All six had called the father and been called by him. None of them were relatives. I could not get a feel for who they were just by call logs. I needed more than just a name.

"I'll get Rominger to run quick backgrounds on each of them," I said. "Driving and arrest records, home address. You check their credit and see if we can get banking information. Put it all together and see if something pops out at us."

It took a while, but one name stood out as clear as day. This person's employment was with the shell company in Delaware that Mr. Leslie had set up to hide shady transactions. He was clean otherwise, but it was obvious that he would have the other secret phone. We had something to question Kate's father with, something he couldn't dance around. I called Rominger right away.

"I'll pick you up at seven in the morning," he said. "It's four hundred miles to Nags Head. We should be there mid-afternoon."

"Are we spending the night or turning around and driving all the way back?"

"Prepare to spend the night if we can get a room," he said. "Likely have to go back to the mainland for that, but it will be a long day otherwise."

"Got it," I said. "I'll be ready."

The person of interest was Brian Belmonti. Upon further investigation, we learned that he was a pilot. He had previously worked for Atlas Air, primarily carrying freight. Mr. Leslie brought him into his circle fifteen years ago. I didn't know the ins and outs of his business dealings, but having your own personal pilot could certainly come in handy. On the other hand, Kate's last known location was at an airport. This Belmonti fellow could have taken her on a private flight to anywhere in the world, maybe even on his own plane. I asked Brody to look into aircraft ownership or leases for either Belmonti, Kate's father, or any of his businesses.

I used my phone to find his social media accounts. He was pushing fifty, but still handsome. He was well-groomed and sporting expensive clothing and accessories. There was one picture of him in front of a 747, but it wasn't recent. I tried to make a connection between him and the nineteen-year-old daughter of his employer but could find none.

"Excuse me, Brody," I said. "You're a woman, and I assume you were once a teenage girl. Could she manipulate this man into rescuing her from a bad situation?"

"More likely daddy sent his errand boy to bail her out," she said.

"He's been around for fifteen years," I said. "Most of her life. Could be some romantic angle."

"Could be," she said. "But my money is on him taking orders from his boss."

"So now we're not trying to track a clueless teenager," I said. "We're trying to track a knowledgeable adult. Makes it a little tougher."

"Let me find out what vehicles he owns," she said. "Get it to the FBI."

"Good stuff," I said. "Now we're into planes, trains, and automobiles."

"And Greyhound buses for all we know."

With help from both the Highway Patrol and the FBI, we collected the vitals on Belmonti. He owned a newer black Lexus with North Carolina plates. That information was plugged into Big Brother. If his car was seen on any of the cameras in the nationwide closed-circuit system, we'd be alerted. He also owned a small plane, which was housed at the Charlotte Douglas International Airport. Someone was sent to lay eyes on the aircraft. The man owned a home near the airport as well. Highway Patrol would keep an eye on the place. We also learned that Brian Belmonti owned a large piece of property in east Tennessee, ostensibly for hunting. No building permits had been issued for the land. A quick scan on Google Earth didn't reveal any buildings, but it was heavily wooded. A small shack could be hidden in any number of places. I tried to look for signs of tracks or a crude driveway, but the resolution wasn't good enough to tell. Google apparently had little interest in updating wilderness lands.

We knew that Belmonti's company phone had pinged a tower in Bristol, not far from the property that he owned. Kate's car had been located at the airport twenty minutes to the south of Bristol. My first instinct was that hunting property. If Belmonti ever spent much time there, he'd have some type of shelter. No cameras would spot them. My gut told me that's where they were, but first I had to talk to Kate's father. Once we presented him with the evidence, there was a chance, he would end all the mystery right then and there.

Brody was still researching and making phone calls when I turned in for the night. She had Tennessee's version of Highway Patrol on the lookout for a certain black Lexus. I hadn't ventured very far into our neighboring state. Other than a trip to Roan Mountain and an episode in the Cherokee Forest, I wasn't familiar with the area. I wasn't familiar with Nags Head either, but after a six-hour drive the next day I was staring at the Atlantic Ocean from Mr. Leslie's vacation home. Rominger took the lead until we got past the introductions and were offered a seat.

"You still haven't heard from your daughter?" I asked.

"No we haven't," he said. "It's not unusual, but you have us worried. Can you tell us what this is all about?"

"After you tell us about Brian Belmonti," I said. "What's is your relationship with him?"

"He's been my right-hand man for many years," he said. "What's Brian got to do with my daughter?"

"Our question exactly," I said.

"I'm not following," he said. "Is my daughter in some kind of trouble?"

"Kate is the number one suspect in a murder investigation," I said.

"That's preposterous," he said. "Impossible."

"She's on the run from law enforcement," I told him. "We have reason to believe that she is with Belmonti. Has he been in contact with you?"

"He asked for some time off," he said. "Some type of family trouble."

"That family is your daughter," I said. "As best we can determine."

I looked in his eyes and saw anguish. He wasn't part of the scheme. He honestly didn't know about any of it. He wrung his hands together and worked his jaw, not knowing what to make of what I'd just told him.

"I'm having a hard time believing any of this," he said. "My little girl. My best friend. This is not happening."

"Maybe you can help us," I said. "We need to get her into custody before she gets hurt or disappears from your life forever."

"I don't know anything about any of this," he said. "I don't think I can process it."

"Your daughter's car was left at the Tri-Cities Airport south of Bristol," I said. "A phone belonging to your company pinged a tower in Bristol. Belmonti owns property just east of there. You can see where I'm headed with this."

"What's going to happen to her?"

"That's not for me to decide," I told him. "We're just trying to find her."

"What do you want me to do?"

"Call Belmonti," I said. "Find out where he is. Don't say anything about Kate."

He called Brian's personal phone, but it went straight to voicemail. He tried the company phone, but it was turned off as well.

"He may not have a signal if he's out in the boonies," he said.

Rominger gave the man his card.

"If he contacts you, we need to know," Rominger said. "Same rules apply. Get his location without scaring him away. Understood?"

"I'll try," he said.

"What kind of man is Brian?" I asked.

"I've trusted him for a long time," he said. "He's like part of our family. He watched Kate grow up. He comes to our house for Christmas and birthdays."

"He may be just trying to assist your daughter," I said. "His motives are misguided, but he may not understand what he's gotten himself into. Don't give up on either of them just yet."

"Please find her," he said. "Tell me that she's safe."

"We're doing our best," Rominger said. "Sorry to break the news to you this way."

"I've got to call my wife," he said.

"We're going," I said. "Thank you for your cooperation. I'm sorry too."

Rominger and I both agreed that Kate's father was telling us the truth as he knew it. We saw no signs of deception during the interview. We did not know if Belmonti was on a romantic mission or not, but I was closer to winning my bet with Brody as to his motives. I needed to get to that Tennessee property as quickly as possible. Rominger wanted to get a room and drive back the following day, but I vetoed the suggestion.

"I've got a comfortable bed and a pretty woman to sleep with six hours from here," I explained.

"Not every day I have the chance to stay in a hotel on the company dime," he said.

"I'll put you up at the Super 8 in Boone if you like."

"Thanks, but I'll pass," he said. "Let's go home."

It was late when I got back to the cabin, but Brody was hard at work. She finished her call and greeted me with a hug.

"Belmonti's plane has not moved," she said. "He hasn't been at his house in Charlotte."

"My hunch is looking more and more accurate," I said. "Daddy didn't send him to rescue Kate either. He was clueless."

"The Lexus hasn't been spotted," she said. "We got his cards into the system too. Not used anywhere since before Kate took off."

"I'm going to Tennessee as soon as I can get my shit together," I told her.

"What about the cops?" she asked. "Rominger is supposed to be supervising you."

"He can't operate outside North Carolina," I said.

"Going rogue always gets you into trouble," she said. "You need Tennessee Highway Patrol to go in with you."

"Taking cops up on a mountain gets them killed," I said. "They don't have the skills I have."

"Get their permission then," she suggested. "Have them stage at the gate."

"I don't have any weight over there," I said. "How am I going to get them to cooperate with me?"

"You've forgotten that we're on the good guy's team these days," she said. "You are not an island. Get Rominger and the Chief to call them. Hell, I'll get the FBI to call them."

"Make it so, number one," I said. "If you can arrange it then I'll abide by it."

"Consider it done."

I was tired, but I had a few things to take care of. I called Red and let him follow me out the door. I went to the garage and gathered my mountain Jedi clothing and shoes. I hung them on the bushes beside the driveway to air out. I found my light backpack and tossed it up on the grass. Red brought me the newfound Frisbee, and I launched it up the hill towards the woods. It didn't travel nearly as far as when I'd thrown it downhill. Red had outrun it and had to backtrack to pick it up. He gave me a look as if to express his disappointment in my arm strength.

"Cut me a break, buddy," I said. "It's late, and I'm plum worn out."

I waited for him to re-mark his territory before calling him in. It was an important task that couldn't be ignored.

Brody was again on the phone when we went back inside. She was talking to someone with the Tennessee Highway Patrol and having a bit of an argument. I suppose that they didn't think letting a lowly private detective take the lead on an important case in their jurisdiction was a good idea. I listened to Brody warn them not to approach the property until I arrived on the scene. She hung up and immediately called her contact at the FBI. Someone in Tennessee was about to get an earful. She motioned for me to wait, so I got a beer and listened to her calls to Rominger and the Chief.

When she finished, she dropped her phone on the desk like a performer drops the mic.

"The weight of the world is now explaining that the almighty Breeze will be searching that property," she said. "They are to provide the utmost in cooperation and assistance as the situation requires. They'll be taking orders from you, mountain man."

"You are amazing," I said. "Queen of law enforcement détente."

"I'm more than just a pretty face," she said.

"No argument here."

Brody and Red both came with me to Tennessee. I planned to have them wait at the car. I could call them into action if needed. We carried our two-way radios in case cell service was insufficient. Our rifles were loaded in the car, but also as a precaution. I'd go in with my pistol, without the dog, and try to locate Kate and Belmonti. Once I assessed the situation, I would have to decide what needed to be done next. I also had a half-dozen cops waiting to hear from me. The best case scenario was that I'd find no defenses and no resistance. I could use the cops as my personal army to swoop in and take the pair into custody. The worst case scenario is that Belmonti had some skills and was determined not to be caught. I had to keep an eye out for booby traps and lines of fire. I wouldn't go into battle against a rifle while only armed with a pistol.

If I met strong resistance, I'd regroup and counterattack with more firepower and a better understanding of the battlefield. I was hoping for the first possibility. We'd found no evidence of military experience for Belmonti, but he was a hunter. This was his turf. He likely knew it well. If he'd decided to hide Kate here, he would likely present some pushback. There was no point in defending a stronghold if you weren't willing to defend it when attacked.

The cops were all standing around drinking coffee and eating doughnuts when we arrived. We went through all the introductions and instructions. The officers gave my questionable garb strange glances. I didn't feel the need to explain myself. It was time to move like smoke and put an end to Kate's journey. If all went as planned, she'd be sleeping on a prison cot tonight. Brody had to restrain Red on his leash when I slid through the fence and started my trek. He wanted to come with me. If I flushed out Kate and Belmonti and caused them to flee, I might have to return to get Red. I didn't want that to happen. I was always shy about involving him when gunfire was a possibility. He was a great tracker, but stealth was not his strong suit. I'd miss out on finding them before I'd let him get shot.

Sixteen

Belmonti's Lexus was of the four-wheel drive variety, but the terrain in front of me seemed too rugged for a luxury car. I picked up on some knobby tire tracks inside the fence that were definitely not made by a Lexus. Those tracks soon disappeared. I had hundreds of acres of steep, rocky and heavily wooded ground to cover. My mission suddenly felt impossible. What was I thinking? I had all those cops at my disposal. Why not sweep over the place like a horde of insects until we found the fugitives?

The possibility that Belmonti was armed and would take action against his pursuers was still very real. This was hunting land, possibly stocked with weapons and ammunition. I was being sent in to locate the hideout, assess the situation, and make the call after that. If there was no threat, I'd simply walk in and bring the targets out for cops to cuff. If I needed an army, I'd call it in, but first I had to find them. I had hoped to find fresh tire tracks again, but that didn't happen. Recent rains must have washed them away. I looked up the hill, trying to guess where this man would build his hunting cabin, shack, tent, or whatever he had for shelter.

The direct route up was impossible for most vehicles to traverse. He must have driven around the rise to more hospitable terrain. Going around on foot would take too long and leave me more vulnerable. I decided on a direct path up through the trees and rocks. Maybe I could see more once I got to the top. My senses gradually increased as I gained elevation. As always, I listened to the sounds. I smelled the earthen scents of dirt and flora. I carefully planted each step while at the same time looking as far ahead as the growth would allow.

It was that time of spring when even the latest bloomers were on full display. The rhododendrons were showing every imaginable shade of pink. There was green everywhere. My khaki outfit was a compromise. It was perfect camouflage during fall and winter, but now I had to be careful not to allow myself to stand out against the full colors of spring. I kept climbing, putting one foot in front of the other continuously. I saw no house and no people. I saw no sign of man's presence on this side of the mountain. I smelled no perfume or deodorant. After several hours, still not to the top, I stopped to rest and think.

It was clear that Kate and Belmonti were not on this side of the mountain. I was going to have to go up and over to find them. I drank some water, chewed on a piece of jerky, and took the weight off my aching knees. I didn't move for twenty minutes. The climb had been a taxing one, and I wasn't getting any younger. I didn't want to go into a confrontation on weary legs. Thinking about going down the other side made me feel a little better. I stopped again at the top of the rise where I had a panoramic view of the surrounding valleys. I still couldn't see any type of dwelling. I hadn't considered the possibility of some sort of hidden bunker that would be difficult to find. I was second guessing that now. I should at least be able to find the car or truck they used to get up here.

Nothing that I could see, hear, or smell, gave me any clue as to which way to look. I picked a random direction and started my descent. I assumed I was closer now, so I tried to move with more stealth. I crept downward, from tree to tree and rock to rock. I paused frequently to listen and smell the air. I swept my eyes back and forth, up and down. I kept thinking that I'd see something at any minute, but an hour passed with nothing found. I had to assume that I'd chosen my direction poorly. There was a lot of land I hadn't seen. He could still be below me, but I could see pretty far down the slope. There was nothing to indicate a shelter down there.

Instead of continuing downward, I started on a horizontal path along the mountainside. I moved back towards the wilderness and away from the road. I kept on that track until I was almost halfway around. Any further and I'd be back on the face that I'd climbed originally. I didn't see a damn thing. Disgusted and tiring, I stopped for another break. It was mid-afternoon, and so far I'd been wasting my time. A quarter of the mountain was left to search, not counting the lower reaches. I cautioned myself not to get sloppy. Blundering about was a good way to get shot. I had enough experience in the High Country to have seen bullets flying in my direction. I'd been lucky early on, but gained experience with each mission. I was still alive, and I wanted to keep it that way.

I backtracked at a lower elevation and began my search of the so far unseen section of the mountain. I still had some daylight left, but my hopes were growing dim. I thought of Brody and Red still waiting down below. I wondered if the cops had given up on me and gone home. I decided to turn on my radio and let someone know what was going on.

"You there, Brody?"

"We're all still here," she said. "I was beginning to worry."

"I'm fine but I haven't found shit," I said. "I'm starting to think this is a dead end."

"How much longer?"

"Two hours or so," I said. "I'm working my way down."

"Roger that," she said. "Stay safe."

As much as I tried to move like smoke, my body wasn't cooperating. The hike to the top had taken its toll. I had another hour of walking to get back to Brody, but I couldn't continue safely. I had to stop again. I found a place to conceal myself and curse my aging bones. It also gave me time to consider that Kate and Belmonti just might not be out here. Where else could they have gone? They didn't drive a Lexus up this mountain, but it had not been spotted by Big Brother anywhere in the country. They hadn't used a credit or debit card at any business establishment or ATM. They hadn't made a phone call from any device that we were aware of. They'd managed to vanish in the age of endless surveillance, although this part of the country was light on cameras.

It was possible that they were somewhere in eastern Tennessee where technology hadn't caught up with the times. How we were going to find them now was the question. I was pretty sure they weren't anywhere near where I was sitting. I would have sensed them. I would have seen, smelled or heard something. I felt strong enough to continue, but when I stood up, my knees complained loudly. They'd had enough climbing for one day. *Stay with me knees — one more hour to go.*

I was limping badly by the time I reached Brody and Red. They both came through the fence as soon as they saw me approaching. The cops were all in their cars, dozing.

"They're not up there," I told Brody. "There is no cabin or anything like shelter that I found."

"Sit in the car," she said. "I've got some Advil in my purse."

I sat in the passenger seat and swallowed four pills. Red nuzzled my ears and neck from the back seat. I turned to him as far as my stiff body would allow and rubbed his ears.

"We'll get them next time, boy," I said.

If he could talk, he would have reprimanded me for not taking him with me.

Brody cut the troopers loose and got behind the wheel. She looked at me with concern.

"Long ass day," she said. "You going to be all right?"

"A beer and a whiskey would help."

"Home it is," she said. "Maybe a hot bath too."

"Sounds good right about now," I said. "Sorry to keep you waiting so long."

"Me and my new cop friends ran out of things to talk about," she said. "Red fetched a stick about a thousand times. He should sleep good tonight."

"Me too," I said. "I should have walked around the mountain and slowly gained altitude. The climb up killed me."

"A little too gung ho maybe," she said.

"My brain is still figuring out that I'm no spring chicken," I said.

"That would be a tough climb for a twenty-year-old," she said.

"I appreciate you saying so," I said. "But I may need you to help me get out of the car."

By the time we got to the cabin, my knees were in total revolt. I used the car for a handhold until I got close to the door. Brody let me lean on her for the last few feet. The steps were an obstacle I couldn't overcome. She opened the door, and I crawled into the kitchen. Red whimpered and licked my face.

"I'm sorry," I said to Brody. "But please help me up."

"What can I do for you?"

"Get me to the couch," I said. "Bring me a beer and a bottle of whiskey."

"Come on, mountain man," she said. "You can do this."

With her help, I made it to the couch. I soon had the booze within easy reach. I put my feet up and commenced to drinking. I could hear water running in the tub. I knew it would help, but I dreaded the walk to the bathroom. It was a big whirlpool model, so it took a while to fill. One beer and three shots emboldened me. I carried the whiskey with me and asked Brody to bring me another beer. I eased myself down into the hot water until I was submerged up to my chin. The jets hit me from every direction. I hadn't taken a real bath in many years. This tub was Brody's territory, but I was grateful that she recommended it for my ailments.

I sat there until the water cooled. My second beer was empty, and I was now six shots into my whiskey bottle. The pain was less, but now my legs were noodles. I was embarrassed to have Brody drag my sorry ass out of the tub and into the bedroom. The last thing I remember is a gentle kiss on the forehead.

"I love you, Brody," I said. "You're the best."

Kate came to me in a dream that night. She was supermodel pretty and wearing sexy lingerie. I lusted after her, but before I could reach her, my knees gave out. I resorted to crawling until a pretty little high heel shoe pushed me off the top of the spillway. I lay broken on the rocks below, looking up at her.

"You're too stupid and disgusting to live," she said.

Then she was gone. I was suddenly wide awake, gasping for air. As usual, Brody was there for me.

"What was it?"

"Kate pushed me off the spillway," I said, skipping the part about lusting after a teenager.

"You think she's winning," Brody said. "That she will win."

"I was too buzzed to think at all when I fell asleep," I said. "But she is somehow evading us."

"She can't stay underground forever," she said. "There are more people involved in this than just you. She'll surface soon."

"I was hoping that you and I would find her," I said. "This has been our case from the beginning."

"You drove the Chief to reopen it," she said. "You created a witness when we had none. You flushed out the culprit and sent her on the run. I don't know what else you can expect to accomplish on this one."

"Right now I need to accomplish a piss," I said. "Help me up."

I grabbed her arm and she pulled me out of bed and to my feet. I stood there for a few seconds, testing my balance. I proceeded to hobble to the bathroom without assistance.

Both knees were red and swollen. I grabbed some Ibuprofen and chugged down some water. I was able to make it back to the bed, but I felt like a ninety-year-old with arthritis.

"What do you think the deal is with your knees?"

"I abused them when I was younger," I said. "The mountains are making me pay."

"Do you want to see a doctor?"

"I do not," I said. "But you might want to get some more Advil soon."

"And beer and whiskey."

"I love how you understand me," I said. "Sorry to wake you."

"Your dreams usually have some significance," she said. "Not that I know what they mean when they happen."

I had a good idea what the dream meant, but I didn't care to discuss it at three in the morning. It wasn't just losing Kate and Belmonti; it was a sign of my lost youth. I wasn't going to have a young beauty like her ever again. Coming home on ruined knees reinforced the fact that I was getting old. I had peaked and was now coming down the other side of aging. I'd always been in good shape, but due to my habits I wasn't necessarily healthy. Dream Kate represented all the girls of the younger Breeze, none of whom would take a second look at me now. Getting old hadn't crept up on me, it showed up suddenly on that mountain in Tennessee.

On the plus side, I had Brody. She was vibrant and attractive and committed to me through thick and thin. I have to say that it was worth more to me at this point in my life than all the sweet young girls I'd ever known. Maybe somehow I'd sensed that this day would come. That's why I'd settled down with Brody. I wished that I could take credit for such a smart decision, but that's not really what happened. I'd been smitten with her since her eyes first twinkled at me in a bar in Fort Myers Beach. I didn't trust her. I'd even tried to run away from her at first, but she persisted. I'm glad that she did. I needed her now more than ever.

I thanked God above for her before falling back to sleep. I was a lucky man, regardless of the condition of my knees. They didn't hurt so badly in the morning, but I went straight for the anti-inflammatories before coffee. I took my cup out on the porch and listened to the hum of the creek. A bright red cardinal came to one of Brody's feeders, not worried about my presence. I tried to remember what a visit from a cardinal meant. Then I remembered an old legend. The cardinal represented a loved one who had passed away. They are supposed to show up when you most need them. I remembered my wife, Laura. Like Brody, she had been my world. Her death devastated me and set off a chain of events that had somehow led me to where I was now. I recalled her fondly, realizing that over time I'd thought about her less. It took many years to move on from her death, but I couldn't be in a better place. Life works out, sometimes in strange ways. *Shit works out, Breeze.*

Brody came out to join me, scaring the cardinal away. It was just as well. Laura and Brody were not in the same place in time.

"Good morning," I said. "Rise and shine."

"You feeling okay this morning?"

"I'm good, thank you," I said. "Love you."

"Angling for breakfast are we?"

"Wasn't my intention, but now that you mention it," I said.

"Let me wake up first," she said. "What's on our agenda for today?"

"Sit here and wait for someone to call and say they've found Kate and Belmonti."

"You've suddenly discovered patience?" she asked.

"I'm not climbing any mountains is what I mean."

"You want me to take Red out?"

"I hate to ask," I said. "But would you?"

"I can't throw a Frisbee like you can," she said. "But I'll do my best."

She left me alone with the creek sounds. The babbling had a calming effect that soothed me. I needed to refill my cup, but I couldn't break the spell of the moment. It was almost hypnotizing. Our three deer friends showed up on the other side of the driveway, nibbling at the new spring shrubs. That was comforting too. This was home now. My old boat was fading from my memory just as Laura had. Time marches on. The clean running water of the creek had replaced the quiet coves of the Florida coast. I was at peace with it all.

I made it through half the day without stressing over finding Kate. The FBI had been alerted to an attempted transaction at the Johnson City DMV. Highway Patrol located Belmonti's car in the parking lot soon after. A man had tried to transfer the title and get new tags, but it was not Brian Belmonti. The man was taken into custody, but he told the cops that he'd paid cash for the car that very morning. He had no bill of sale and was still being held at the Fall Branch Highway Patrol Office. I was offered to opportunity to speak with the man.

Fall Branch was sixty-five miles from the cabin. The drive took an hour and a half. The man in police custody was Tony Delgatto. He looked like a bit player in the Sopranos. His hair was slicked back and greasy. He had several gold chains around his neck. He'd had enough cash on his person to buy an expensive Lexus. He claimed the deal was legit.

"Where did you meet the man who sold you the car?" I asked.

"At the Double Tree in Johnson City," he said.

"Was there a girl with him?"

"Sweet young thing," he said. "Didn't get her name."

"How did the subject of the car come up?"

"You know, Belmonti, Delgatto," he said. "We just naturally got to talking."

"An Italian thing?"

"Something like that," he said. "He was in a jam, so I helped him out. I bought the car for almost what it's worth."

"What's your business, Mr. Delgatto?"

"Import and export," he said. "Dabbling in fine automobiles."

"Stolen cars?"

"I didn't steal the car," he said. "You think a Lexus owner leaves a signed title in the glove box?"

"Okay, so you paid cash straight up for the car," I said. "Was Belmonti staying at the hotel?"

"Maybe he was poaching the free breakfast," he said. "I met him in the dining area."

"Were you staying at that hotel?"

"I had a date," he said. "Carried on late, so I spent the night. What's going to happen to my car?"

I looked to the Highway Patrol Officer that let me in to talk to this guy. He apologetically stated that the vehicle would be held as evidence. Once the case was cleared, Delgatto could claim it. He assumed that Belmonti would confirm the legitimate sale once he was in custody. Other officers were on their way to the DoubleTree Hotel. Delgatto asked if he was free to go. The officer offered him a ride home. He said he had another car still at the Double Tree, so I offered for him to ride with us. He didn't stick around once we parked. He got into a Hummer and drove off immediately.

Two officers were leaving just as we went inside. We explained who we were and asked what they'd learned. Kate and Belmonti were gone. They had used the girl's fake ID to check in, paying with cash.

"What was the name on the ID?" I asked.

"Leslie Jones," he said. "Twenty-one years old from Charlotte, North Carolina."

"I'll get it to the FBI," Brody said.

"Closing in but a step behind," I said. "Where would they go from here?"

"With a pocket full of cash," she said. "But no car."

"They can buy another car," I said. "How do we zero in on that?"

"If I were them I'd buy from a private seller," she said. "Get a car that still had valid tags."

"They could have used the hotel's computer to search Craigslist," I said.

"I can check the computer's history to see where they've been on the internet," she said.

"Good thinking."

We went in to talk to the clerk about checking the guest computers. They were wary about our request, so I asked if there were any rooms available. We ended up checking in. As paying guests, the computers were ours to use. The bill was just over a hundred bucks, and I was tired anyway. There were two computers in a small room adjacent to the pool. We each sat down and started checking the recent history. It took only minutes for Brody to hit on Craigslist car searches.

"Here's a Honda Civic," she said. "I bet that's our car."

"What else?"

"A beater and a VW," she said. "Kate's not riding in either."

"Call the Civic seller."

The car had been sold that very afternoon. The buyer paid in cash and left with the tag, promising to return it as soon as they transferred the title. The description matched Kate and Belmonti. The transaction had taken place in Johnson City, just a few miles from the DoubleTree. They'd arrived in an Uber and didn't haggle. The Uber transaction had not alerted Big Brother. I asked the seller what the tag number was. He didn't recall. He'd written them a bill of sale but didn't keep a copy for himself. I got his name and number before driving to the DMV. A helpful clerk was able to give us the tag number. That too was given to the FBI. There was nothing else for us to do that day.

We drove back to the hotel and tossed ourselves on the bed. I was beginning to think that this Belmonti fellow was pretty sharp. He'd managed to stay one step ahead of not just us, but the FBI too. He understood the basic principles of avoiding detection. I had to admire him for that, but I was sure he'd screw up eventually. Unless he bought a boat and disappeared into the swamps of Florida, he would show up on someone's radar. Having the girl with him limited just how far he could go underground. She wouldn't tolerate a mosquito-infested hellhole like Brody, and I had once done. We had spent weeks deep in the Everglades to avoid detection. Kate would want a hot shower every day and all the basic comforts of home. They would not guess that we had learned what car they were driving. They would let their guard down. They would pass a license plate reader or go through a toll booth, and the cops would have them. All we had to do was wait.

Seventeen

After a brief rest, we drove around town until we found a place that sold beer. We picked up a pizza to go with it and took our loot back to the hotel. Brody turned on the local news, on the off chance that our fugitive couple would appear. They did not, but there was plenty of crime to report on in the Tri-City area. I stopped short of criticizing the high crime rate of the greater Bristol area when I remembered we were there to catch a murderer from Banner Elk. Of course, she'd been imported from Charlotte, which had its own crime problem. The Keys and the sleazier stops along the coast of Florida were also riddled with drugs and criminal activity of every flavor. It was a good thing we had a secluded cabin to shield us from the wicked ways of the outside world.

I stood in front of the window and opened the curtains, imagining all the drug deals, muggings, and auto thefts that were taking place within sight of the hotel. I closed the curtains to shut it all out. I wanted no part of that world. Brody was watching some detective show that I knew would ultimately reveal that the husband had killed his wife, either for insurance money or because he had another woman. All of it was depressing. I wanted to go home. Then I remembered that we'd left Red alone in the house.

"We've got to go," I said.

"I was just getting settled," she said. "It's late."

I'm not settled," I said. "And Red is back at the cabin wondering what the hell happened to us."

"Shit," she said. "How could we forget?"

"Our minds are otherwise occupied," I said. "Do you mind if we just go home now?"

"It's only a little over an hour away," she said. "I guess it's not too late."

"Good, let's blow this popcorn stand."

Red was busting a gut at the back door when we arrived. He didn't want our attention, he only wanted to get outside. He burst through the door and barely made it to the first bush. I could almost hear him sigh as he shot a stream at the shrubbery that lasted for several minutes.

"Sorry, buddy," I said. "But thanks for holding it."

He scolded me with one sharp bark. Then followed me back into the cabin. I gave him some loving in apology for forgetting about him. I was soon forgiven. It was good to be home. Brody handed me two Advils and a beer. I went out to the porch with Red in tow to sit in peaceful solitude. Heavy fog had settled into the holler, and it felt like rain. I was absent-mindedly rubbing one knee when Brody joined us.

"They still swollen?" she asked.

"No, just feels like sandpaper rubbing when I move."

"I'll look into some natural remedies," she said. "You want some balm or something in the meantime?"

"That shit doesn't work," I said. "Don't believe the commercials."

"You'd rather stick with whiskey and ibuprofen," she said.

"It might be temporary, but my regimen provides relief."

"And rots your liver," she said.

"It's not my liver that hurts."

"It will catch up to you one of these days," she said. "Just like your knees."

"I appreciate the advice, nurse Brody."

"I'd appreciate you sticking around for a long time," she said. "I'm just trying to take care of you."

"You're probably right about the whiskey," I said. "But it tastes so good. The buzz is pleasant."

"Goofball," she said.

"Nurse Ratched," I said.

"Cuckoo's Nest, right?" she said. "Great movie."

"For twenty years I thought her last name was Ratchett," I said. "Don't remember how I learned the proper name."

"I thought you said Rachett."

"Ratched," I said. "Look it up."

"I love wasting time with you," she said. "We can just be ourselves."

"Wait," I said. "We've had a scientific discussion on the benefits of whiskey for pain relief, and a cinematic debate about one of the most important supporting characters in movie history. That's deep stuff if you ask me."

"Have another whiskey, mountain man," she said. "I'm going to take a shower."

"Need any help?"

"Not tonight," she said. "I'll be ready for bed soon."

"Me too," I said. "Meet you under the covers."

In an effort to prevent her from showing up in my dreams, I tried not to think about Kate. I focused on Belmonti instead, a man I'd never met. In all of his pictures, he had an air of confidence about him, like he held some power. I knew that the real power came from Kate's father, his boss. Mr. Leslie had called him his right-hand man. Brody had alluded to him being an errand boy. Which was it? Was he a fixer that provided vital service to his employer, or was he a well-paid gopher? The pay and benefits had to be excellent to hire him away from his previous position as a commercial airline pilot. I wondered what Kate's father had his fingers in besides his obvious business dealings. Having a pilot on the payroll could mean drug running, or it could simply be a way to travel privately instead of commercial. The only plane in the picture belonged to Belmonti, though, not his boss.

There was a thread there that I couldn't unravel. I needed more information. I wasn't going to get it lying in bed, but I wasn't keen to get up either. I was warm and cozy. Brody's body heat and the sound of her breathing were comforting. I let it all slip away and dozed off. I didn't dream about Kate. I saw Brian Belmonti for a fleeting second, but then he was gone. I tried to run after him, but my legs wouldn't cooperate. I slowed to a stop. I saw myself bent over with my hands on my knees. Belmonti was gone.

The need to pee woke me well before daylight. I carefully extracted myself from the covers, trying not to wake Brody. It took two steps to verify that my knees still didn't care to get with the program. I found a container of Tiger Balm sitting in front of the coffee maker, Brody's subtle reminder. I sat at the table and rubbed the goo all over both knees. It smelled like menthol and cloves. When there was enough coffee brewed to fill a cup, I took my coffee to the porch. Red was still sleeping in front of the fireplace, even though there was no fire burning. A strong wind had blown the fog away. It was still warm, but there was energy in the atmosphere like a storm was approaching. My knees tingled from the Tiger Balm, but it was no instant cure. I took a quick assessment of my other body parts. The back was okay, as were my neck and shoulders. My feet didn't hurt; neither did my hips. Elbows, ankles, and wrist all checked out. Other than the knees, I was pain-free. I needed to rest them so they could recover from my ill-fated climb up a Tennessee mountain.

There were no birds at the feeder or deer in the yard, so I snuck quietly back to the kitchen for a second cup of coffee. I wasn't quiet enough to fool Red. He scratched on the door to go outside. I let him roam free, not feeling up to playing fetch. He'd scratch again when he was ready to come back in. I sat at the desk and turned on the computer, not really knowing what I was looking for. After ten minutes I was ready to buy some turmeric for my knees, or maybe some glucosamine and chondroitin, or maybe both. The Tiger Balm wasn't doing shit.

I clicked through what I could find about Mr. Leslie. It was mostly impersonal corporate stuff with a smattering of civic involvement mixed in. His public persona was squeaky clean, but we knew of at least one shell company that he'd set up. We knew he used a secret phone to communicate with Belmonti. There had to be more that we'd failed to uncover. What concerned me was the fact that I had looked the man in the eyes and deemed him to be telling the truth. He said he knew nothing about what was going on concerning Kate. Had I been wrong? Rominger thought he'd been honest too. Had we both been wrong? If I allowed for that possibility, a completely new range of scenarios presented itself. Was the father involved in Kate's attempted escape? Was Belmonti keeping her hidden until dad could take over and whisk her off to an island somewhere? He appeared to have enough money to pull it off. I was driving myself crazy with all the potential new paths this investigation could take. I needed Brody's input.

The only proper way to wake a sleeping beauty is with the smell of bacon cooking. It worked like a charm. She couldn't be mad at me when I put a plate of bacon between us.

"Eggs coming up," I said. "You want toast?"

"Just coffee," she said. "Lots of coffee."

I didn't start the day's work until she was fully awake. I let Red back in and fed him too. When the time was right, I told Brody about my new fears.

"You said the father was on the up and up," she said.

"Now I'm worried he wasn't."

"Why?"

"Just a hunch," I said. "Belmonti doesn't do anything without his boss's approval. That's his livelihood. Would he betray his boss and best friend to go on the run with the teenage daughter?"

"Stranger things have happened," she said. "I told you about teenage girls, especially pretty ones."

"She gives him some of that sweet thing, and he loses his mind?"

"Did you ever see American Beauty?" she asked.

"Middle-aged guy falls for a teenage hottie," I said. "Does silly stuff to try to impress her."

"Sound familiar?"

"I suppose it does," I said. "But how can I dig deeper into Kate's father?"

"Leave it to me, Mr. Computerphobe," she said. "I'll see what I can find out."

What she did was send a request to her contact at the FBI. If you wanted to dig deep into an international businessman's life, the Deep State was the place to turn. Not even the IRS could break down a man's personal and business transactions like the FBI. They could work with the NSA and even the CIA to uncover every skeleton and shady endeavor a person could imagine. Brody was told that it would take time, but the work would begin soon. Now we were waiting on the fugitive couple to surface and for the dirt on Mr. John Leslie. Being forced to sit and wait wasn't the worst thing that could happen to my knees.

I mentioned my brief research on the topic to Brody. She wanted to drive to town to pick up these alleged remedies. I knew doing nothing all day would bore me to death, so I agreed to ride to Walmart in Boone in search of turmeric and other goodies. I used a shopping cart like a walker, cleverly disguising my infirmity. A man's got to have some pride. Brody talked to the pharmacist and selected supplements based on his recommendations. I noticed that each was the most expensive option, but let it pass. I was willing to try just about anything at that point. I would gladly rattle some chicken bones and offer a rum sacrifice to Jobu in exchange for some relief.

I asked to stop at the ABC store while we were in Boone. I still had some whiskey left, but there was no point in taking any chances. Then we remembered ibuprofen, which we hadn't bought at Walmart. We stopped at

Walgreens to make that purchase. I waited in the car while Brody went inside. I was not taking well to feeling like a crippled person. This was something new to me. I said a little prayer that it wouldn't last long and that I'd return to my former self soon.

That was the first day in a while that we weren't on the phone or computer all day trying to chase down clues as to Kate's whereabouts. It was late in the afternoon when Brody got a call from her friend at the FBI. John Leslie was law-abiding for the most part, but there was one curious tidbit in his financial history. He did what most successful businessmen did, which was move his money around to lessen his tax burden. He took advantage of every legal loophole available to him. He ran major purchases through his bogus Delaware company to avoid sales tax. He capitalized and amortized and invested. The odd item on his list was a business holding in Grand Cayman, which allowed him to open a bank account offshore. He regularly transferred legally earned and already taxed funds to that Cayman account. It was perfectly legal, but now outside the reach of the IRS.

"Why would someone hide money offshore if it was legally obtained?" I asked.

"In the event his accounts are frozen for some as yet unknown infraction, he'll have a tidy little nest egg that he can still access," came the reply.

"So we can assume there is some hidden wrongdoing that we don't know about yet, or a plan to commit some fraud in the future," I said.

"We cannot assume anything. So far, it appears, he's stayed within the letter of the law."

"I'd assume that if Mr. Leslie suddenly disappeared that we could find him in Grand Cayman."

"That would be a reasonable guess."

"What about extradition?" I asked.

"Although autonomous, they are technically still a British Territory, so our agreements with Great Britain apply."

"That's good to know," I said. "Anything else odd about this man?"

"Still digging, but we've added his autos, and credit cards to our watch list. If he moves, we'll know it."

"Thanks," I said. "That may turn out to be helpful. Kate's fake ID name is being watched too, right?"

"Yes, sir."

Daddy had some money stashed in the islands. Daughter was still underground, with daddy's employee. If the father was in on the plan to help Kate escape, he'd have to make a move soon. If Kate and Brian were a romantic couple, dad wouldn't stand for it. Which was it? If the father wasn't involved, the two fugitives would have to go ever deeper to avoid detection. They'd need new identities. They'd have to go someplace far away where they weren't known. They'd have to have money. If the father was going to help them avoid detection, how would he do it? He certainly had the money and the means to assist them, but did he have the motive? A third option then presented itself. What if the father did not approve, but planned to solve the problem himself? If someone who had benefitted so greatly from his relationship with me ran off with my daughter, I'd want to kill him. I might forgive my daughter but not the friend. The problem, in this case, was that Kate had killed someone. It was no accident either. That's tough for anyone to forgive. I didn't know John Leslie well enough to decide where his head was on this. He'd been outwardly upset. His surprise and regret seemed genuine.

"Help me out here, Brody," I said. "I'm thinking in circles."

"You don't know which side the father is on," she said.

"Right," I said. "I can't believe that he fooled me so thoroughly, if that's what happened."

"Try this," she said. "He didn't know, yet. He was genuinely taken aback, but now he's recovered and had time to think about it. He'll step in and save the day for his daughter somehow."

"Plausible," I said. "How can we get in front of whatever he's planning?"

"I don't see how we can," she said. "Other than to be ready to move on a moment's notice. One of the three will show up on a camera or use a credit card, and we'll be on them."

"The cops will be on them," I said. "We'll be sitting here playing pinochle."

"We don't play pinochle," she said.

"Okay, backgammon."

"What's wrong with the cops picking them up?"

"Nothing," I said. "I'm being selfish."

"You think you're owed a final showdown?"

"Of course not," I said. "It would be nice to put the finishing touch on this case is all."

"We're not cops," she said. "It's not our job. In fact, we can drop the whole thing any day now. We've done our part."

"Like hell," I said. "I'm going to make some calls. I want us to be there when these two knuckleheads go down."

"Suit yourself."

I called Rominger, the Chief, and Angelina. I told them all to call me immediately upon a sighting of the fugitives. I'd head in their direction as soon as I got the call. I wouldn't interfere with law enforcement, but I'd be there to help if my services were required. All three agreed to notify me, which made me feel a little better. I even vowed to lay off the booze until this thing was over. I wanted to be sharp if and when I got the call. It's not always easy doing the right thing, but sometimes you have to make the sacrifice.

The only thing that happened over the next two days was John Leslie leaving Nags Head and returning to Charlotte. His wife stayed at the beach. She had not been a subject of our investigation in any manner. She'd been a ghost, out of the picture. Kate must have been daddy's little girl, and not as close with her mother. Maybe she could manipulate him as well as she'd been directing Belmonti. I asked Brody to look into the mother a little deeper. Maybe we were missing something about her.

Speculating about the motives of all the players gave me something to do. Most times, given enough information, I could prod my gut to lead me in one direction or the other. This time, I didn't know enough. Anything could happen. I needed to be on my toes, as much as my knees would allow. They were improving, but slowly. I hadn't put them to the test, and I didn't want to anytime soon. I even took it easy when running Red in the backyard. He didn't hold it against me, but he sensed that something was different about our playtime. I was grateful for his leniency.

Kate and Belmonti had to be somewhere in eastern Tennessee. Kate's father was at home in Charlotte. Her mother was in Nags Head. Brody and I, along with multiple law enforcement agencies were waiting for any of them to make a move. Something had to give soon. I tried to relax and heal, but there was tension caused by the waiting. The waiting is always the hardest part. This wasn't a man in the woods that I could track down. I had to rely on others to get the job done. Some faceless person at the FBI would get an alert, hopefully interpret it properly, and sound the alarm. The closest police department would get the call. Neighboring agencies would respond as well. Someone involved in that initial response would call me. Depending on where the action took place, Brody and I would attempt to be there. That's how I played it through in my mind. That's how I wanted it to go down. There was a better likelihood that we would find out of Kate's arrest long after it happened. We'd be happy that she was in custody, but it would be a letdown that we didn't get to participate.

Eighteen

Most citizens don't realize our government's capabilities when it comes to surveillance and detection. The TV series *Hunted* gave us a glimpse into that power by highlighting ways in which fugitives can be found. Contestants were given short notice and had to disappear from the radar for twenty-eight days to have a chance to win a quarter-million dollars. Most were woefully unprepared. A team consisting of former intelligence agents proved more than capable of using the technology available to them to track down the players without difficulty.

Matt and Christina began running in Mount Pleasant, South Carolina. They withdrew one-hundred dollars at an ATM near a bus station and proceeded to buy tickets to board a bus to Atlanta, where they were captured after only one day on the run. Miles and Will began running in Atlanta, Georgia. A "Have You Seen Me?" campaign by the investigators on social media produced a tip (by the sister of the woman currently helping them) which led the investigators to track the movements of the sister's cell phone as she was driving the contestants to South Carolina. A flying drone found them on a boat. They made it fifteen days before being captured. Sentra and Thu began running in Woodstock, Georgia. They immediately withdrew money from an ATM and purchased a burner phone. The investigators were able to determine the purchase location and time, with which they were able to get the receipt with the phone number. They began tracking the phone's movements until the couple was captured.

If the government wants to find you, they will. You can't use a credit or debit card. You can't use a cell phone. You can't drive past a CCTV camera on an interstate or toll booth. You can't trust that those helping you won't give you up. I knew about all of this from personal experience. It's the reason I hate having phones and a computer. It's the reason

I never had a checking account or a credit card. I had a good reason at the time to avoid government detection. I doubted that Kate and Belmonti fully understood this concept, but somehow they'd managed to stay hidden so far. We'd come close with the guy they sold the Lexus to, but it didn't pay off. My money was on the FBI though. They would be found. I was just getting tired of waiting for it to happen.

In the meantime, my knees were feeling better each day. I was no longer in constant pain. They still felt a little fragile, but the improvement was obvious. Red seemed to appreciate me being more like my old self. Brody made sure I took the turmeric daily. I tried to drink more water. I hadn't drunk any booze in a week. The lack of alcohol in my blood stream was enough to want this mission to be over. It was harder to fall asleep at night without it. I resorted to taking an over the counter sleep aid. The booze worked better.

I knew that this case could break at any minute, and I wanted to remain mentally sharp. I read to break the boredom, waiting on the call. Brody had put our packs loaded with provisions in the car. Our weapons were clean and loaded. Our two-way radios were charged and ready, as was the handheld GPS. Even Red seemed anxious, sensing that something was about to go down. He was ready too.

It all happened at once. We didn't get one call, but several. I answered the Chief, while Brody talked to Rominger.

"Deputy Will is in pursuit of our suspects," he said. "221 heading north from Linville Falls."

"What's the plan?"

"We're setting up on 184," he said. "Highway Patrol is sending units to all Blue Ridge Parkway entrances. Avery County is sending cars ahead of Will to as many intersections as they can."

"We're on the road," I said. "Update me as you can."

"Rominger is setting up on 105 just east of the liquor store," Brody said. "Hold on; it's the FBI."

Mrs. Leslie had just purchased a ticket at the airport in Norfolk bound for Charlotte. Her husband simultaneously purchased four seats on an American Flight to Grand Cayman out of the same airport. Kate and Belmonti were attempting to outrun a patrol car. They'd left Tennessee by some circuitous route but were soon spotted in North Carolina. The rush to set up roadblocks was haphazard. The key to catching them was Angelina staying within sight and directing other assets to intercept. One of those assets would be Brody and me.

On the spur of the moment, I decided to take Red with us. We hauled ass down McGuire Mountain towards Banner Elk. We sped through town, knowing that the police would all be forming a roadblock somewhere in front of us. Before we reached them, we got another call. The chase had turned onto 105 north and was heading towards the Grandfather Country Club. I made a quick visual in my mind of the network of roads in the area. 105 continued on to Boone where they could pick up 321 south to Charlotte. Rominger's location was the most likely one to encounter the fugitives. That's where I wanted to be. I called the Chief.

"Coming through your position from town," I said. "Joining Highway Patrol on 105."

"Proceed with caution," he said.

We zipped through the three cars that Banner Elk had managed to assemble on 184. We hung a left at the light onto 105 and soon encountered a more substantial gathering of cops. Two officers on foot were allowing a slow line of traffic beyond the checkpoint, closely inspecting each car. I immediately noticed a flaw in where they had set up. If Belmonti and Kate saw them, they could turn left at the light, but then the Banner Elk PD would have them. What they could do is make a sudden right onto Profile Trail Road. It didn't really go anywhere, but served as an access to Grandfather Mountain. It was a popular hiking destination. It was also where some deer poachers had parked before climbing up and hunting out of season. I knew the trail well.

"Call Rominger," I told Brody. "Quick. Tell him we're going to the Profile Trail entrance."

As soon as she finished, I made a hard U-turn, squealing tires and blowing smoke. As soon as the car straightened up, we were facing a head-on collision with a certain Honda Civic. Belmonti was behind the wheel. He took the only route left available to him. The one that I knew he would take. It started as a blacktop road but soon eroded into gravel. There was no outlet. I was practically touching his bumper, pushing him to make a mistake. That's when I saw him stick a pistol out of the driver's side window. I hit the brakes just as he fired wildly over his shoulder. I let him maintain his distance because there was nowhere for him to go at this point.

Brody produced her handgun and rolled down her window.

"Don't shoot unless you have to," I said. "He's got to stop soon. We can take them down once they're on foot."

Soon the gravel road turned to dirt. Soon after that, there was no road at all, only a parking area. He could either try to spin around in the parking lot or make a run for it. I didn't want to wreck our car if I could avoid it. I urged him to get out and run. Brody and I watched the pair bail out of their car before it came to a complete stop. Red barked. It was go time.

"Stay with the girl," I hollered to Brody. "Come on, Red."

The pair didn't stay together long. Kate was not a runner. She veered off the trail and rushed headlong into the brush, hoping to hide. Brody broke off in pursuit. Red stayed with me. Adrenaline drove me uphill with a purpose. I knew the man was armed, but I was certain he wouldn't last long in an uphill dash. I watched for signs that he was preparing to take cover and shoot. That's what I expected him to do, but it's not what he actually did. He kept running, faster than I was. He was gradually putting distance between us. When I realized that I was losing ground, I also became aware of the awful pain in my knees. It was their fault I wasn't keeping up, but I could not let this man escape me on a mountain. My reputation was at stake. I did my best to ignore the multiple knives stabbing my knees. They felt as if they were filled with broken glass, and every movement caused the glass to grind in the joints. I soldiered on, still falling behind the pace. Belmonti had to tire soon. I had to keep going. This guy was no match for me.

There were forks in the trail ahead of me. If I lost sight of him, I might take the wrong fork. Tears formed in my eyes as I tried to ignore the pain. I started feeling nauseous. Belmonti hadn't quit yet. I was forced to make a terrible choice. Red was still at my side, taking his cues from me. He could be on the runner in a matter of seconds if I gave him the command. He could also get shot. We came to a rise where the trail descended for a stretch before going back up the mountain. Belmonti was at full gallop on his way down. I wasn't going to catch him.

"Take him down, Red," I yelled. "Go get him, boy."

He was off like a cheetah, teeth bared. I slowed to a walk, trying not to collapse on the trail. I pulled out my radio and called Brody.

"I need help," I said. "Send the cops up here."

"Roger that," she said. "One female in custody."

I didn't respond. I tucked the radio in my pocket, sucked in some air and went after

Red. I had all sorts of horrible thoughts about what I would find. I sped up, desperately regretting the command I'd given him. I heard a shot, which gave me the impetus I needed to start running again. I waited for the sound of a dog wailing, but it didn't come. Instead, as I got closer, I heard a low growl. It was something I'd never heard from Red. It was downright mean. I came upon the two of them and took a quick survey. The gun was on the ground, as was Belmonti. His right wrist was bleeding badly. Red had a tight grip on his neck. The look on the man's face was one of pure fear. My loving pet had transformed himself into a vicious wolf. Somehow, he'd managed to disarm his target and completely disable him.

I let him maintain his grip for another minute while I picked up Belmonti's gun and tucked it in my pants.

"Please," Belmonti said. "He's going to kill me."

"Let go, Red," I yelled. "Let him go, boy."

Red looked at me and kept his teeth on the man's neck for another few seconds. He growled again before releasing his hold, warning him not to try anything. He backed up a few steps and maintained an attack posture. That was enough for Brian Belmonti.

"I give up, man," he said. "Call him off."

"Come here, boy," I said.

Red obeyed and came to my side. He sat like a good boy who'd just returned a Frisbee. I kept my weapon trained on Belmonti, but knelt to give him a rub behind the ears.

"Good boy," I said. "Red's a good boy."

It took all of my strength and will not to allow Belmonti to see that I was hurting. I kept pointing my pistol at him while I spoke.

"You're going to bleed out if you don't address that wound on your wrist," I said. "I don't trust you enough to do it myself."

"What do I do?"

"Put pressure on it," I said. "Help is on the way. Press hard."

He followed my instructions. I watched him like a hawk until I heard footsteps coming our way. I didn't take my eyes off him until I saw that it was Rominger and one of his men coming to take over for me.

"He's got a deep puncture wound on his wrist," I said. "Might need a tourniquet."

"You okay?" Rominger asked. "You don't look so good."

"Tend to him first," I said. "I may need some help getting down from here."

Then it all went black.

Nineteen

When I opened my eyes, I thought I was in heaven, but the two angels looking down at me were Brody and Angelina. I struggled to return to reality. I was told to lay still. Someone I didn't recognize began checking my vitals. A big, wet dog kiss is what snapped me out of my fog. Red nuzzled my neck and poked me with his cold nose.

"You still with us, mountain man?" Brody asked.

"I'm alive," I answered. "Kate? Belmonti?"

"Belmonti is on his way to the hospital," Angelina said. "Kate is on her way to jail."

"I guess that's it then," I said.

"Other than getting you off this mountain," Brody said. "It's all downhill if you can walk."

I sat up and asked for some water. I didn't try to stand right away. The two women looked on with concern.

"We could probably get a four-wheeler up here if you want to wait," Angelina said.

"I need something for pain," I said. "Shoot me up and I'll try to make it down."

We all looked to the medic that had checked me out.

"I don't know, man," he said. "You don't have any life-threatening injuries. Morphine isn't indicated in your case."

"It's the pain that caused me to black out," I explained. "We can all sit here until help arrives or you can give me a shot and I'll hopscotch to my car."

"Okay," he said. "I'll do it. Show me your ass."

I managed to roll onto my side and expose one butt cheek. He didn't waste any time, stabbing me quickly and depressing the plunger before I knew what hit me. I was briefly woozy and worried that I'd be too stoned to manage the trek, but the lightheadedness passed. Throughout the next few minutes, I felt a wave of happy juice flow through my body. I could feel the abrasion going on in my knees, but it didn't hurt much.

"Help me up," I said to the women.

"You might want to pull your pants up first," Brody said.

"Shit, thanks," I said. "Good idea."

I fumbled with the button at the top of my jeans until Brody had to step in and help.

"You're going the wrong way, pretty lady," I told her.

"First time for everything," she said.

"Let's see if you can walk," Angelina said.

I tested my legs, carefully and slowly. I couldn't feel much below my waist, but at least I wasn't in excruciating pain. My feet felt like I was wearing Herman Munster shoes. I walked a small circle without falling.

"I'd like to go home now," I announced.

"One step at a time, okay," Brody said. "I'll be right beside you."

"Prettiest trail guide ever," I said. "Both of you."

"Concentrate on what you're doing, lover boy," Brody said.

"Okay, I got this."

I knew that I would pay for it later when the morphine wore off, but the finishing touch on this operation had to be me walking down on my own power. Being carried out of a fight showed weakness. Limping home torn and bloody was badass. My head was a little fuzzy, but I focused on my steps. I kept putting one foot in front of the other, making progress on the trail.

"Not exactly moving like smoke, am I?"

"The mission is complete," Brody said. "It's okay. You're doing good."

"Stubborn son of a bitch, isn't he?" Angelina said.

"He'd walk all the way to the cabin if I let him," Brody said.

"No, no," I said. "The car is far enough."

My knees needed some lubrication. I could feel them creaking like rusty gears. I was likely making them worse with this little stunt, but I'd deal with that later, even if it meant a trip to the doctor's office. All I wanted to do was get home and break my alcohol drought. I could taste the beer and whiskey. I used it as my motivation. To hell with Kate and Belmonti. I was done with this shit.

As the trail widened, we came to a big log lying next to it. I took the opportunity to rest. Red put his head in my lap to comfort me. The medic warned that the morphine would only last so long. I drank some more water and continued, this time with one arm around Brody's shoulders. We were moving slower, but still making progress. We maneuvered a short uphill stretch that really took it out of me. Angelina manned my other side, so I had both arms on a cutie's shoulder. There were worse ways to travel. By the time I could see the car, I was practically being carried by my angels.

Brody opened the back door and told me to lie down. Before I gave up the ghost, I turned to Angelina.
"Thanks for being our friend," I said. "For being there for us both."

"My privilege," she said. "Besides, I know both of you would be there for me."

"I'm going to lay down now."

The door closed and I started to fade. I could hear the two girls talking, but I couldn't comprehend what they were saying. I settled into the rear seat cushions and took a little nap. The next thing I knew I was at home on the couch. Red was in front of the fireplace. I sat up and was immediately handed a beer and a shot of whiskey, followed by three ibuprofen pills.

"You're going to be a hurting pup soon," she warned. "Better get a head start on it."

"You going to join me?"

"Excellent suggestion," she said, popping her own cold beer.

"To catching the bad guys," I said, raising my beer.

"Damn straight," she said, clinking her can against mine.

Twenty

Kate's sorority sisters all turned against her during their interviews with investigators, led by our coerced witness, Rachel. She apologized for alerting Kate and allowing her to run. We apologized for terrorizing her in order to get to the truth. The sorority was disbanded, but none of the sisters faced any legal consequences.

Katherine "Kate" Leslie pled guilty to second-degree murder in exchange for the minimum sentence, which in North Carolina is twelve years. She would be a free person by the age of thirty.

Brian Belmonti was charged with being an accessory after the fact and obstruction of justice. Facing fifteen years in prison, he agreed to a plea deal also. He was sentenced to eight years in prison for his part in harboring Kate and attempting to flee.

Kate's parents were not charged in connection with their daughter's crimes.

Frank and Darla Buck were satisfied that justice had been served. To show their appreciation to Breeze and Brody, an old fashioned country dinner was arranged at their home. During the visit, Frank slipped Breeze an additional five hundred dollars.

Breeze finally agreed to see a doctor. He was told that he had osteoarthritis of the knees. Brody continued to seek alternative remedies, while Breeze insisted that the booze really helps.

Red has been treated like a king since his heroic efforts on Grandfather Mountain. He's still not allowed in the bedroom though.

Author's Thoughts

The real Brian Belmonti is a Boeing 767 captain for Atlas Air. I honored his request to be a character in one of my books. I hope he is pleased, even though in this book Belmonti was kind of a douche.

If you'd like a character named after you, feel free to contact me at Kimandedrobinson@gmail.com
Along with character names, plot suggestions are also welcome.

If you enjoyed this book, please leave a review at Amazon. All reviews are appreciated.

As I finish this episode of the Mountain Breeze Series, spring is almost upon us here in the Blue Ridge Mountains. We survived our first winter, but we are very much ready for warmer weather.

We put out a new bird feeder recently. The first visitor was a male cardinal. I thought it appropriate to include him in this book.

My knees are okay, but the local liquor store keeps running out of my favorite whiskey.

OTHER BOOKS IN THIS SERIES

Banner Elk Breeze
https://amzn.to/2VRCpCV

Blue Ridge Breeze
https://amzn.to/2J8gk1m

Beech Mountain Breeze
https://amzn.to/2UxBCad

More Mountain Breeze Adventures Coming Soon

ED ROBINSON'S PREVIOUS WORKS ALSO STARRING BREEZE

Trawler Trash
https://amzn.to/2Lg4HTL

Following Breeze
https://amzn.to/2fXJgq2

Free Breeze
https://amzn.to/2fXILfv

Redeeming Breeze
https://amzn.to/2gbBjAx

Bahama Breeze
https://amzn.to/2fJiMe6

Cool Breeze
https://amzn.to/2weKg1l

True Breeze
https://amzn.to/2ws6Hzp

Ominous Breeze
https://amzn.to/2HrgMW8

Restless Breeze
https://amzn.to/2O0jGT4

Enduring Breeze
https://amzn.to/2unav5I

Benevolent Breeze
https://amzn.to/2Ccw4uj

Nonfiction by Ed Robinson

Leap of Faith; Quit Your Job and Live on a Boat
https://amzn.to/2CilBh1

Poop, Booze, and Bikinis
https://amzn.to/2JaNTjv

The Untold Story of Kim
https://amzn.to/2u1ah4z

Acknowledgements

Proofreaders:
Dave Calhoun
Jeanene Olson
Laura Spink

Editor:
John Corbin

Cover Design:
https://ebooklaunch.com/

Interior Design:
https://ebooklaunch.com/

Made in the USA
Middletown, DE
14 July 2025